Lonely Planet

COASTAL VICTORIA

ROAD TRIPS

WITHDRAWN

This edition written and researched by

Anthony Ham

HOW TO USE THIS BOOK

Reviews

In the Destinations section:

All reviews are ordered in our authors' preference, starting with their most preferred option. Additionally:

Sights are arranged in the geographic order that we suggest you visit them and, within this order, by author preference.

Eating and Sleeping reviews are ordered by price range (budget, midrange, top end) and, within these ranges, by author preference.

Map Legend

Routes

▨▨▨ Trip Route
▬▬▬ Trip Detour
▨▨▨ Linked Trip
▬▬▬ Walk Route
　　 Tollway
　　 Freeway
　　 Primary
　　 Secondary
　　 Tertiary
　　 Lane
　　 Unsealed Road
✕✕✕ Plaza/Mall
ıııııı Steps
) ꞊ ꞊ Tunnel
꞊꞊꞊꞊ Pedestrian Overpass
- - - Walk Track/Path

Boundaries

- - - International
- - - - State
╤╤╤╤ Cliff
▬▬▬ Wall

Population

✪ Capital (National)
◉ Capital (State)
● City/Large Town
○ Town/Village

Transport

✈ Airport
+⊕+ Cable Car/ Funicular
Ⓟ Parking
+◉+ Train/Railway
Ⓣ Tram
Ⓜ Underground Train Station

Trips

① Trip Numbers
⑨ Trip Stop
🚶 Walking tour
↪ Trip Detour

Route Markers

[M31] [1] National Highway
[A5] [63] State Route

Hydrography

〜 River/Creek
〜 Intermittent River
░ Swamp/Mangrove
〜 Canal
⬯ Water
⬯ Dry/Salt/ Intermittent Lake
░ Glacier

Areas

░ Beach
░ Cemetery (Christian)
░ Cemetery (Other)
░ Park
░ Forest
░ Urban Area
░ Sportsground

Note: Not all symbols shown here appear on the maps in this book

Symbols In This Book

✓ Top Tips
🍷 Food & Drink
🔗 Link Your Trips
🌳 Outdoors
💬 Tips from Locals
📷 Essential Photo
🚗 Trip Detour
🚶 Walking Tour
📖 History & Culture
✗ Eating
👪 Family
🛏 Sleeping

- - - - - - - - - - - - - - - -

⊙ Sights
🛏 Sleeping
🏖 Beaches
✗ Eating
🏃 Activities
🍷 Drinking
🌳 Courses
☆ Entertainment
☞ Tours
🛍 Shopping
✦ Festivals & Events
ℹ Information & Transport

- - - - - - - - - - - - - - - -

These symbols and abbreviations give vital information for each listing:

☏ Telephone number
🐾 Pet-friendly
⊙ Opening hours
🚌 Bus
Ⓟ Parking
⛴ Ferry
⊖ Nonsmoking
🚋 Tram
✳ Air-conditioning
🚆 Train
@ Internet access
apt apartments
🛜 Wi-fi access
d double rooms
🏊 Swimming pool
dm dorm beds
🥗 Vegetarian selection
q quad rooms
r rooms
📖 English-language menu
s single rooms
ste suites
👪 Family-friendly
tr triple rooms
tw twin rooms

CONTENTS

PLAN YOUR TRIP

Welcome to Victoria 5
Coastal Victoria Map 6
Coastal Victoria Highlights 8
Melbourne City Guide 10
Need to Know 12

ROAD TRIPS

1 Great Ocean
Road   5–7 Days   17

2 Gippsland & Wilsons
Promontory   6–7 Days   27

3 Mornington
Peninsula   3–4 Days   35

4 Goldfields
& Macedon   4–5 Days   43

DESTINATIONS

Melbourne 52
Great Ocean Road 79
Torquay 79
Anglesea 81
Lorne 81
Apollo Bay 83
Cape Otway 84

Port Campbell National Park 84
Warrnambool 86
Port Fairy 87
Portland 89
Gippsland 90
Phillip Island 90
Koonwarra 93
Wilsons Promontory
National Park 94
Walhalla 97
Mornington Peninsula 99
Mornington 99
Sorrento 100
Portsea 103
Mornington Peninsula
National Park 103
Flinders 104
French Island 104
Goldfields 106
Woodend 106
Hanging Rock 106
Kyneton 107
Castlemaine 107
Maldon 109
Maryborough 110
Ballarat 111

DRIVING IN
AUSTRALIA 117

Great Ocean Road (p17)

WELCOME TO
COASTAL VICTORIA

Victoria is home to some of the best road trips on the planet. The four trips in this book will take you from its dramatic rugged coastline to its historic and beautiful interior.

From driving along one of the world's most iconic and scenic coastal roads to visiting the vast, historic goldfields from which the state's great wealth originates, from enjoying first-class locally grown food and wine to walking on pristine and near-deserted white-sand beaches, Victoria's paved roads take you on journeys that showcase the extraordinary beauty of the southeast corner of the vast continent of Australia.

Whether your dream is criss-crossing the 'garden' state from sea to mountains, or a more intimate loop along quiet country roads, we've got it covered.

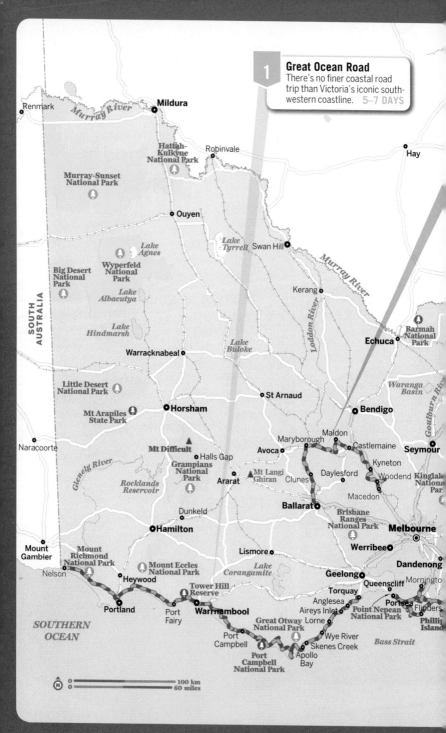

1

Great Ocean Road
There's no finer coastal road trip than Victoria's iconic southwestern coastline. **5–7 DAYS**

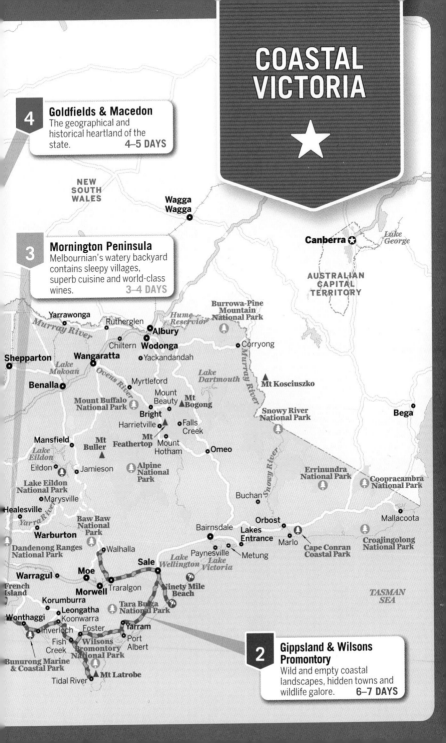

COASTAL VICTORIA

★

4 Goldfields & Macedon
The geographical and historical heartland of the state. **4–5 DAYS**

3 Mornington Peninsula
Melbournian's watery backyard contains sleepy villages, superb cuisine and world-class wines. **3–4 DAYS**

2 Gippsland & Wilsons Promontory
Wild and empty coastal landscapes, hidden towns and wildlife galore. **6–7 DAYS**

NEW SOUTH WALES

Wagga Wagga

Canberra ✪

Lake George

AUSTRALIAN CAPITAL TERRITORY

Yarrawonga
Rutherglen
Murray River
Chiltern **Albury**
Wangaratta **Wodonga**
Yackandandah
Corryong
Hume Reservoir
Burrowa-Pine Mountain National Park
Murray River

Shepparton
Lake Mokoan
Myrtleford
Lake Dartmouth
▲ Mt Kosciuszko

Benalla
Ovens River
Mount Beauty
Bright
Mt Bogong
Snowy River National Park

Bega

Mount Buffalo National Park
Harrietville
Falls Creek
Mansfield
Mt Buller ▲
Mt Feathertop
Mount Hotham
Omeo
Snowy River

Eildon
Jamieson
Alpine National Park
Errinundra National Park
Cooracambra National Park

Lake Eildon
Lake Eildon National Park

Healesville
Marysville
Buchan
Orbost
Mallacoota

Yarra River
Baw Baw National Park
Bairnsdale
Lakes Entrance
Marlo
Croajingolong National Park

Warburton
Walhalla
Cape Conran Coastal Park

Dandenong Ranges National Park
Lake Wellington
Paynesville
Metung
Lake Victoria

Warragul
Moe
Sale
French Island

Morwell
Traralgon
Ninety Mile Beach
TASMAN SEA

Korumburra
Tara Bulga National Park
Leongatha
Koonwarra
Wonthaggi
Inverloch
Foster
Yarram
Port Albert
Fish Creek
Wilsons Promontory National Park
Bunurong Marine & Coastal Park
Tidal River
▲ Mt Latrobe

COASTAL VICTORIA

HIGHLIGHTS

★

AUSTRALIAN SCENICS/GETTY IMAGES ©

RACHEL LEWIS/GETTY IMAGES ©

Twelve Apostles (left) These craggy rock formations are one of Victoria's most vivid sights, and have come to symbolise this stunning corner of the country. See them on Trip 1

Wilsons Promontory (above) Mainland Australia's southernmost point and finest coastal national park, Wilsons Prom is heaven for bushwalkers, wildlife-watchers and surfers. See it on Trip 2

Hanging Rock (right) Sacred site of the traditional Wurundjeri people, Hanging Rock also once served as a hideout for bushrangers. See it on Trip 4

MELBOURNE

Melbourne is one cool city. The culinary and coffee scene is widely considered to be the best and most diverse in Australia, while its arts and sporting scenes lie at the heart of its appeal. Abundant parks, a revitalised riverbank and laneways with attitude round out an irresistible package.

Where to Eat

The city centre and Southbank areas are awash with fabulous restaurants to suit all budgets; yum cha for Sunday lunch in Chinatown is a city institution. Carlton's Lygon St is famous for Italian restaurants, while Fitzroy and Brunswick have astonishing multicultural variety. See p68 for more information.

Where to Stay

Plenty of places in the city centre cover all price ranges and put you in the heart of the action. Other options are more far flung. See p66 for more information.

Getting Around

Some freeways have well-signposted toll sections. The City Loop train line runs under the city, and the City Circle Tram in the CBD is free. Buy a myki Visitor Pack

Centre Place

(www.myki.com.au; $14) for one day's travel and discounts on various sights. The myki card can be topped up at 7-Eleven stores and myki machines at all train stations and some tram stops in the city centre.

Parking

Most street parking is metered ($3.20 to $5.50 per hour); avoid the signposted 'Clearway' zones. There are plenty of (expensive) parking garages in the city; rates vary and some have cheaper weekend deals. See p117 for more information on driving.

Useful Websites

Broadsheet Melbourne (www.broadsheet.com. au) The best eating, drinking and shopping spots.

Good Food (www.goodfood.com.au) Restaurant and foodie happenings around Melbourne.

That's Melbourne (www.thatsmelbourne.com. au) Downloadable maps, info and podcasts.

Three Thousand (www.thethousands.com.au/melbourne) A weekly round-up of local goings on.

Tourist Information

Melbourne Visitor Centre (MVC; Map p58; ☏03-9658 9658; www.melbourne. vic.gov.au/touristinformation; Federation Sq; ⏱9am-6pm; ☏; ☒Flinders St) has comprehensive tourist information on Melbourne and regional Victoria, including excellent resources for mobility-impaired travellers, and a travel desk for accommodation and tour bookings. There are power sockets for recharging phones, too.

NEED TO KNOW

FUEL

Unleaded and diesel fuel widely available. Prices vary from $1.20 in cities to $2.20 in the outback. Distances between fill-ups can be long in the country.

IMPORTANT NUMBERS

Emergencies ✆ 000

International Access Code ✆ 0011

INTERNET ACCESS

Wi-fi is widespread in urban areas, less so in remote Australia. For public wi-fi locations, visit www.freewifi. com.au. There are relatively few internet cafes; try public libraries.

MOBILE PHONES

European phones work on Australia's network, but most American and Japanese phones won't. Use global roaming or a local SIM card and prepaid account. Telstra has the widest coverage.

RENTAL CARS

Avis (www.avis.com.au)

Budget (www.budget. com.au)

Europcar (www.europcar. com.au)

Hertz (www.hertz.com.au)

Climate

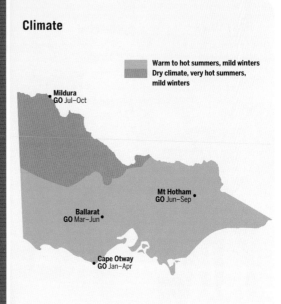

Warm to hot summers, mild winters

Dry climate, very hot summers, mild winters

Mildura GO Jul–Oct

Mt Hotham GO Jun–Sep

Ballarat GO Mar–Jun

Cape Otway GO Jan–Apr

When to Go

High Season (Dec–Jan)

》 Beaches are packed with local holidaymakers soaking up the sun and enjoying school holidays.

》 Easter and June/July school holidays are also busy times.

》 Book months ahead for coastal accommodation, including camping.

Shoulder Season (Feb–Mar)

》 Quieter time with many more accommodation vacancies.

》 Late-summer weather can be particularly hot.

Low Season (Apr–Nov)

》 Milder weather; often decent rainfall during second low season of September to November.

》 July to September is peak whale-watching season off Warrnambool.

》 Ski-resort high season from June to August.

Daily Costs

Budget: Less than $125

» Hostel dorm bed: $25–$50 a night

» Simple pizza or pasta meal: $15–$25

» Short bus or tram ride: $4

Midrange: $125–$280

» Double room in a motel, B&B or hotel: $100–$200

» Breakfast or lunch in a cafe: $20–$40

» Short taxi ride: $25

Top End: More than $280

» Double room in a top-end hotel: from $200

» Three-course meal in a classy restaurant: $120–$150

» Tickets to an event: $100–$250

Eating

Cafes Good for breakfasts and light lunches.

Restaurants International and mod-Oz cuisine.

Pubs Well-priced bistro food.

Roadhouses No-nonsense outback meals.

Vegetarians Wide choice in cities, less so elsewhere.

Eating price indicators represent the cost of a standard main course:

$	less than $15
$$	$15–$32
$$$	more than $32

Sleeping

B&Bs Often in restored heritage buildings.

Campgrounds & Caravan Parks Most have sites and simple cabins.

Hostels Buzzing budget digs with dorm beds.

Hotels From simple to upmarket.

Motels No-frills but fine for a night.

Sleeping price indicators represent the cost of a double room with private bathroom in high season:

$	less than $100
$$	$100–$200
$$$	more than $200

Arriving in Melbourne

Melbourne Airport (Tullamarine)

Bus SkyBus services run 24 hours a day to the city ($18 one-way, 20 minutes), leaving every 10 to 30 minutes.

Taxi A taxi into the city costs around $40 (25 minutes).

Avalon Airport

Bus Avalon Airport Bus meets every flight and takes passengers to Melbourne ($22, 40 to 50 minutes).

Taxi A taxi to Melbourne costs around $80 (one hour), or $50 to Geelong (20 minutes).

Money

ATMs are widespread, but not off the beaten track or in some small towns. Visa and MasterCard are widely accepted, Diners Club and Amex less so.

Tipping

It's common (but not obligatory) to tip in restaurants if the service warrants it; to 10% is the norm. Round up taxi fares.

Opening Hours

Banks ⊙9.30am-4pm Monday to Thursday, until 5pm Friday

Cafes ⊙7am-4pm or 5pm

Petrol stations & roadhouses ⊙8am-10pm

Pubs ⊙noon-2pm and 6-9pm (food); drinking hours are longer and continue into the evening, especially Thursday to Saturday

Restaurants ⊙noon-2pm and 6pm-9pm

Shops ⊙10am-5pm or 6pm Monday to Friday, until either noon or 5pm on Saturday and (in major cities and tourist towns) Sundays

> For more, see Driving in Australia (p117).

Road Trips

1 Great Ocean Road, 5–7 Days
There's no finer coastal road trip than Victoria's iconic southwestern coastline. (p17)

2 Gippsland & Wilsons Promontory, 6–7 Days
Wild and empty coastal landscapes, hidden towns and wildlife galore. (p27)

3 Mornington Peninsula, 3–4 Days
Melbournians' watery backyard contains sleepy villages, superb cuisine and world-class wines. (p35)

4 Goldfields & Macedon, 4–5 Days
The geographical and historical heartland of the state. (p43)

Point Nepean National Park (p105)
FILEDIMAGE/GETTY IMAGES ©

Great Ocean Road

1

One of the most beautiful coastal road journeys on earth, this world-famous road hugs the western Victorian coast, passing world-class beaches, iconic landforms and fascinating seaside settlements.

TRIP HIGHLIGHTS

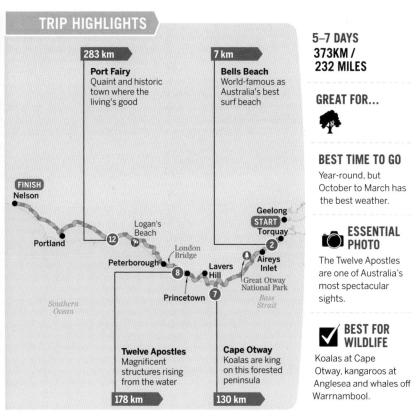

283 km

Port Fairy
Quaint and historic town where the living's good

7 km

Bells Beach
World-famous as Australia's best surf beach

FINISH
Nelson

Portland

Logan's Beach

London Bridge

Peterborough

Lavers Hill

Princetown

Great Otway National Park

Southern Ocean

Bass Strait

Geelong
START
Torquay

Aireys Inlet

Twelve Apostles
Magnificent structures rising from the water

178 km

Cape Otway
Koalas are king on this forested peninsula

130 km

5–7 DAYS
**373KM /
232 MILES**

GREAT FOR...

BEST TIME TO GO
Year-round, but October to March has the best weather.

ESSENTIAL PHOTO
The Twelve Apostles are one of Australia's most spectacular sights.

BEST FOR WILDLIFE
Koalas at Cape Otway, kangaroos at Anglesea and whales off Warrnambool.

Left Twelve Apostles (p23)

1 Great Ocean Road

The Great Ocean Road begins in Australia's surf capital Torquay, swings past Bells Beach, then winds its way along the coast to the wild and windswept koala heaven of Cape Otway. The Twelve Apostles and Loch Ard Gorge are obligatory stops before the road sweeps on towards Warrnambool with its whales, and Port Fairy with its fine buildings and folk festival, before the natural drama peaks again close to the South Australian border.

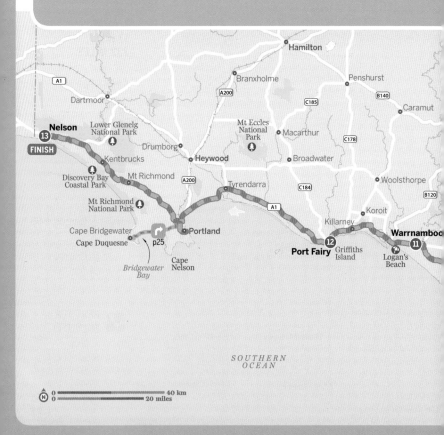

❶ Torquay (p79)

The undisputed surfing capital of Australia is a brilliant place to start your journey. The town's proximity to world-famous Bells Beach, and status as home of two iconic surf brands (Rip Curl and Quicksilver) have assured Torquay's place at the pinnacle of mainstream surf culture. Torquay's beaches lure everyone from kids in floaties to backpacker surf-school pupils. **Fishermans Beach**, protected from ocean swells, is the family favourite. Ringed by shady pines and sloping lawns, the **Front Beach** beckons lazy bums, while surf lifesavers patrol the frothing **Back Beach** during summer. Famous surf beaches include nearby **Jan Juc** and **Winki Pop**. Visit the **Surf World Museum** (p79), home to the Australia's Surfing Hall of Fame, then start

🔗 LINK YOUR TRIP

3 Mornington Peninsula

Do the trip in reverse to finish in Torquay, from where it is just a short drive to Queenscliff to catch the Queenscliff–Sorrento Ferry to Sorrento (p38).

4 Victoria's Goldfields

Where Trip 4 ends in Ballarat, it's an 87km drive down the Midlands Hwy to the Geelong bypass, and from there it's around 30km into Torquay.

working on your legend by taking surf lessons with **Westcoast Surf School** (☏03-5261 2241; www.westcoastsurfschool.com; 2hr lesson $60) or **Torquay Surfing Academy** (☏03-5261 2022; www.torquaysurf.com.au; 34a Bell St; 2hr group/private lessons $60/180).

✗ 🛏 p80

The Drive ❱❱ Pass the turn-off to Jan Juc, then take the next left (C132) and follow the signs to Bells Beach.

TRIP HIGHLIGHT

② Bells Beach (p80)

A slight detour off the Great Ocean Road takes you to famous Bells Beach, the powerful point break that is part of international surfing folklore (it was here, albeit in name only, that Keanu Reeves and Patrick Swayze had their ultimate showdown in the film *Point Break*). When the right-hander is working, it's one of the longest rides in the country. If you're here just to look, park in the car park and head for the lookout, from where stairs lead down to the beach (not for swimming).

The Drive ❱❱ Return to the Great Ocean Road (B100), and soon after doing so consider taking the turn-off to spectacular Point Addis, a vast sweep of pristine beach. Anglesea is a further 10km down the Great Ocean Road, with dense woodland lining the road as you descend into town.

③ Anglesea (p81)

Mix sheer orange cliffs falling into the ocean with hilly, tree-filled 'burbs and a population that booms in summer and you've got Anglesea, where sharing fish and chips with seagulls by the Anglesea River is a decades-long family tradition for many. **Main Beach** is good for surfers, while sheltered **Point Roadknight Beach** is for families. In addition to such quintessentially Australian summer pastimes, Anglesea is famous for those seeking to spy their first kangaroos – at **Anglesea Golf Club** (☏03-5263 1582; www.angleseagolfclub.com.au; Noble St; 9 holes from $25; ⏱clubhouse 8am-midnight) you can watch kangaroos graze on the fairways.

✗ 🛏 p81

The Drive ❱❱ The B100 follows the coast (although it does sidestep attractive Point Roadknight) for 11km to Aireys Inlet, and then to Fairhaven, with a historic lighthouse and wonderful beaches. From Aireys it's 18km of glorious coast-hugging road into Lorne – stop for photos at the Great Ocean Road memorial archway.

④ Lorne (p81)

There's something about Lorne... For a start, this is a place of incredible natural beauty, something you see vividly as you drive into town from Aireys Inlet: tall old gum trees line its hilly streets,

---

GREAT OCEAN ROAD FESTIVALS

Falls Festival (www.fallsfestival.com; 2/3/4-day tickets $320/390/433; ⏱Dec 28-Jan 1) A four-day knees-up over New Year's on a farm just out of town, this stellar music festival attracts a top line-up of international rock and indie groups. Past headliners include Iggy Pop, Spiderbait, Kings of Leon and the Black Keys. Sells out fast, and tickets include camping.

Port Fairy Folk Festival (www.portfairyfolkfestival.com; tickets $75-290; ⏱Mar) Australia's premier folk-music festival is held on the Labour Day long weekend in March. It includes an excellent mix of international and national acts, while the streets are abuzz with buskers. Accommodation can book out a year in advance.

Rip Curl Pro (www.aspworldtour.com) Since 1973, Bells has hosted the Rip Curl Pro every Easter. The world championship ASP tour event draws thousands to watch the world's best surfers carve up the big autumn swells, where waves have reached 5m during the contest! The Rip Curl Pro occasionally decamps to Johanna Beach, two hours west, when fickle Bells isn't working.

and Loutit Bay gleams irresistibly. Kids will love the beachside swimming pool, trampolines and skate park, and there's more than 50km of bushwalking tracks around Lorne. Up in the hilly hinterland behind town, seek out the lovely **Erskine Falls** (Erskine Falls Access Rd); it's an easy walk to the viewing platform, or 250 (often slippery) steps down to its base. Back in town, the **Great Ocean Road National Heritage Centre** (15 Mountjoy Pde; ⊙9am-5pm) tells the story of the construction of the Great Ocean Road.

✕ 🛏 p82

The Drive ›› Although the winding nature of the road makes it feel longer – by now you know the deal: dense forests to your right, uninterrupted sea views to your left – it's just 20km from Lorne to Kennett River.

❺ Kennett River

Kennett River is one of the easiest places to see koalas in Australia. In the trees immediately west of the general store and around the excellent caravan park, koalas pose (well, they're often asleep) in the tree forks, sometimes at eye level. Local parrots and lorikeets are also known to swoop down and perch on heads and outstretched arms if you stay still enough.

The Drive ›› The road could hardly get closer to the coast for the 22km from Kennett River into Apollo Bay.

🡒 DETOUR:
BRAE AT BIRREGURRA

Start ❹ Lorne

Dan Hunter is one of Australia's most celebrated chefs and he single-handedly put rural Dunkeld on the map with his fantastic Royal Mail Hotel. Thus the Birregurra tourism team must've been licking their lips when they heard he was moving to their town to open his new restaurant. **Brae** (🕿03-5236 2226; www.braerestaurant.com; 4285 Cape Otway Rd, Birregurra; 8-course tasting plates per person $180, plus matched wines $120; ⊙noon-3pm Fri-Mon, from 6pm Thu-Sun) takes over from the much-loved Sunnybrae, with its farmhouse getting a refit by renowned architects Six Degrees. The restaurant uses whatever is growing in its 12 hectares of organic gardens. Reservations are essential, well in advance. It all happens in the small historic town of Birregurra, 38km from Lorne on the way to Colac.

❻ Apollo Bay (p83)

At Apollo Bay, one of the Great Ocean Road's largest towns, rolling hills provide a postcard backdrop to the town, while broad, white-sand beaches dominate the foreground. Local boy Mark Brack, son of the Cape Otway Lighthouse keeper, knows this stretch of coast better than anyone around – both his **Otway Shipwreck Tours** (🕿0417 983 985; msbrack@bigpond.com; 3hr tours adult/child $50/15) and **Mark's Walking Tours** (www.greatoceanwalk.asn.au/markstours; 2-3hr tour adult/child $50/15) are outstanding. Another worthwhile excursion is the kayak expedition out to an Australian fur seal colony in a double kayak with **Apollo Bay Surf & Kayak** (🕿0405 495 909; www.apollobaysurfkayak.com.au; 157 Great Ocean Rd; 2hr kayak tours $65, 1½hr surf lessons $60).

✕ 🛏 p83

The Drive ›› The turn-off for Lighthouse Rd (ie Cape Otway), which leads 12km down to the lighthouse, is 21km from Apollo Bay. Those 12km are through dense woodland pretty much all the way.

TRIP HIGHLIGHT

❼ Cape Otway (p84)

Cape Otway is the second most southerly point of mainland Australia (after Wilsons Promontory) and this coastline is particularly beautiful, rugged and historically treacherous for passing ships despite the best

WHY THIS IS A GREAT TRIP

ANTHONY HAM
WRITER

Whenever I have visitors from overseas, the first place I take them is the Great Ocean Road. What makes it a classic is the winning combination of stunning natural beauty and world-famous attractions lined up along the roadside like a string of pearls – Bells Beach, koalas at Cape Otway, the Twelve Apostles, Loch Ard Gorge...and they're just the beginning.

Top: Loch Ard Gorge (p24)
Left: Koala
Right: Cape Otway (p21)

efforts of the **Cape Otway Lightstation** (☏03-5237 9240; www.lightstation.com; Lighthouse Rd; adult/child/family $19.50/7.50/49.50; ⊙9am-5pm). The oldest surviving lighthouse on mainland Australia, it was built in 1848 by more than 40 stonemasons without mortar or cement. The forested road leading to Cape Otway is a terrific spot for koala sightings. Where are they? Look for the cars parked on the side of the road and tourists peering up into the trees.

🛏 p84

The Drive » The road levels out after leaving the Otways and enters narrow, flat scrubby escarpment lands that fall away to sheer, 70m-high cliffs along the coast between Princetown and Peterborough – a distinct change of scene. The Twelve Apostles are after Princetown.

- - - - - - - -

TRIP HIGHLIGHT

❽ Twelve Apostles (p84)

The most enduring image for most visitors to the Great Ocean Road, the Twelve Apostles jut from the ocean in spectacular fashion. There they stand, as if abandoned to the ocean by the retreating headland, all seven of them... Just for the record, there never were 12, and they were once called 'Sow and Piglets' until some bright spark in the 1960s thought they might attract tourists with a more venerable name. The two stacks on the eastern

(Otway) side of the viewing platform are not technically Apostles – they're Gog and Magog. And the soft limestone cliffs are dynamic and changeable, with constant erosion from the waves: one 70m-high stack collapsed into the sea in July 2005 and the Island Archway lost its archway in June 2009. The best time to visit is sunset, partly to beat the tour buses, and to see little penguins returning ashore. For the best views, take a chopper tour with **12 Apostles Helicopters** (☎03-5598 8283; www.12apostleshelicopters.com.au; 15min flights $145).

The Drive » When you can finally tear yourself away, continue northwest along the Great Ocean Road and in no time at all you'll see the signpost to Loch Ard Gorge.

9 Loch Ard Gorge (p84)

Close to the Twelve Apostles, Loch Ard Gorge is a gorgeous U-shaped canyon of high cliffs, a sandy beach and deep blue waters. It was here that the Shipwreck Coast's most famous and haunting tale unfolded: the iron-hulled clipper *Loch Ard* foundered off Mutton Bird Island at 4am on the final night of its long voyage from England in 1878. Of 37 crew and 19 passengers on board, only two survived. Eva Carmichael, a non-swimmer, clung to wreckage and was

PORT CAMPBELL TO WARRNAMBOOL

The Great Ocean Road continues west from Port Campbell, passing **London Bridge**...fallen down. Now sometimes called London Arch, it was once linked to the mainland by a narrow natural bridge. In January 1990 the bridge collapsed, leaving two terrified tourists marooned on the world's newest island – they were eventually rescued by helicopter.

The **Bay of Islands** is 8km west of tiny **Peterborough**, where a short walk from the car park takes you to magnificent lookout points.

The Great Ocean Road officially ends near here, where it meets the Princess Hwy (A1).

washed into a gorge, since renamed Loch Ard Gorge, where apprentice officer Tom Pearce rescued her. Despite rumours of a romance, they never saw each other again and Eva soon returned to Ireland. There are several walks in the area taking you down to the cave where the shipwreck survivors took shelter, plus a cemetery and rugged beach.

The Drive » It's around 6km along the B100 from Loch Ard Gorge into Port Campbell.

10 Port Campbell (p85)

Strung out around a tiny bay, Port Campbell is a laid-back coastal town and the ideal base for the Twelve Apostles and Loch Ard Gorge. Its has a lovely, sandy, sheltered beach, one of few safe places for swimming along this tempestuous stretch of coast.

✕ ⌂ p85

The Drive » There is a feeling of crossing a high clifftop plateau on the first stretch out of Port Campbell. After the Bay of Islands, it turns inland through green agricultural lands.

11 Warrnambool (p86)

Warrnambool means whales, at least between May and September, when whales frolic offshore on their migration. Southern right whales (named due to being the 'right' whales to hunt) are the most common visitors, heading from Antarctica to these more temperate waters. Undoubtedly the best place to see them is at Warrnambool's **Logan's Beach whale-watching platform** – they use the waters here as a nursery. Call ahead to the visitor centre to check if whales are about, or see www.visitwarrnambool.com.au for latest sightings. Otherwise, take the time to visit the top-notch **Flagstaff**

Hill Maritime Village

([☎]03-5559 4600; www.
flagstaffhill.com; 89 Merri St;
adult/child/concession/family
$16/6.50/12.50/39; [⏰]9am-
5pm), with its shipwreck
museum, heritage-listed
lighthouses and garrison,
and its reproduction of
a historical Victorian
port town. It also has
the nightly **Shipwrecked**
(adult/child/family $26/14/67),
an engaging 70-minute
sound-and-laser show telling the story of the *Loch
Ard*'s plunge.

[✕] [📖] p86

The Drive >> The road (the
Princes Hwy (A1), and no longer
the Great Ocean Road) loops
around to Port Fairy, just 29km
from Warrnambool.

- - - - - - - - - - - - - -

`TRIP HIGHLIGHT`

⑫ Port Fairy (p87)

Settled in 1833 as a whaling and sealing station,
Port Fairy retains its

historic 19th-century
charm with a relaxed,
salty feel, heritage
bluestone and sandstone
buildings, whitewashed
cottages, colourful fishing
boats and wide, tree-
lined streets; in 2012 it
was voted the world's
most liveable community.
Across the bridge from
the picturesque harbour,
Battery Hill has cannons
and fortifications. To
guide your steps through
the town's heritage, pick
up a copy of the popular
*Maritime & Shipwreck
Heritage Walk* from the
visitor centre. And there's
a growing foodie scene
here too – **Basalt Wines**
([☎]0429 682 251; www.basalt
wines.com; 1131 Princes Hwy;
[⏰]11am-4.30pm Sat & Sun),
just outside Port Fairy in
Killarney, is a family-run
biodynamic winery that
does tastings in its shed.

[✕] [📖] p88

The Drive >> The road hugs
the coast into Portland (75km)
and then the traffic lessens as
you leave the main highway and
drive northwest along the C192
for 67km into Nelson.

- - - - - - - - - - - - -

⑬ Nelson

Tiny Nelson is the last
vestige of civilisation
before the South Austral-
ian border – just a general
store, a pub and a handful
of accommodation places.
We like it especially for its
proximity to the mouth of
the **Glenelg River**, which
flows through **Lower
Glenelg National Park**.
The leisurely 3½-hour
trips run by **Nelson
River Cruises** ([☎]0448
887 1225, 08-8738 4191; www.
glenelgrivercruises.com.au;
cruises adult/child $30/10;
[⏰]Sep-Jun) head along
the Glenelg River and
include the impressive
**Princess Margaret Rose
Cave** ([☎]08-8738 4171; www.
princessmargaretrosecave.
com; adult/child/family
$17.50/11.50/40; [⏰]hourly
tours 11am to 4.30pm, reduced
hours winter), with its
gleaming underground
formations – along this
coastline of towering
formations, these ones at
journey's end are surely
the most surprising. If
you prefer to explore
under your own steam,
contact **Nelson Boat &
Canoe Hire** ([☎]08-8738
4048; www.nelsonboat
andcanoehire.com.au).

**↱ DETOUR:
CAPE BRIDGEWATER**

Start: ⑫ Port Fairy

Cape Bridgewater is an essential 21km detour off
the Portland–Nelson Rd. The stunning 4km arc
of **Bridgewater Bay** is perhaps one of Australia's
finest stretches of white-sand surf beach. The road
continues on to **Cape Duquesne**, where walking
tracks lead to a spectacular **Blowhole** and the eerie
Petrified Forest on the clifftop. A longer two-hour
return walk takes you to a **seal colony** where you can
see dozens of fur seals sunning themselves on the
rocks; to get a little closer, take the exhilarating **Seals
by Sea tour** ([☎]03-5526 7247; www.sealsbyseatours.com.
au; adult/child $35/20; [⏰]Aug-Apr), a 45-minute zodiac
cruise to see Australian and New Zealand fur seals.

Gippsland & Wilsons Promontory

2

This loop through Victoria's southeast takes you from wild coastal landscapes to a semi-abandoned mining town hidden deep in the forest.

TRIP HIGHLIGHTS

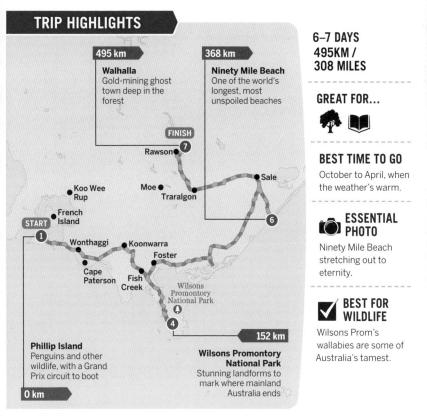

495 km
Walhalla
Gold-mining ghost town deep in the forest

368 km
Ninety Mile Beach
One of the world's longest, most unspoiled beaches

FINISH
7 Rawson

Moe ● **6**
Traralgon
● Sale

● Koo Wee Rup

● French Island

START
1

● Wonthaggi ● Koonwarra
Foster

Cape Paterson
Fish Creek

Wilsons Promontory National Park

4

152 km

Phillip Island
Penguins and other wildlife, with a Grand Prix circuit to boot

0 km

Wilsons Promontory National Park
Stunning landforms to mark where mainland Australia ends

6–7 DAYS
495KM / 308 MILES

GREAT FOR...

BEST TIME TO GO
October to April, when the weather's warm.

ESSENTIAL PHOTO
Ninety Mile Beach stretching out to eternity.

BEST FOR WILDLIFE
Wilsons Prom's wallabies are some of Australia's tamest.

2

Gippsland & Wilsons Promontory

Traversing one of Australia's most underrated corners, this journey southeast and east of Melbourne takes in the wildlife and wild landscapes of Phillip Island and Wilsons Prom, and engaging rural towns such as Inverloch, Koonwarra and Port Albert, before almost falling off the map in the ghost town of Walhalla on your way back to Melbourne.

TRIP HIGHLIGHT

❶ Phillip Island (p90)

It may cover barely 100 sq km, but Phillip Island sure crams a lot in. For most visitors, Phillip Island means the nightly arrival of the penguins at the Penguin Parade, one of Australia's great wild-life spectacles. It doesn't happen until sunset, so wildlife-lovers will want to fill in the afternoon with a visit to Seal Rocks and the Nobbies, home to the country's largest

colony of fur seals, and the Koala Conservation Centre. The island's coast is the domain of swimmers and surfers, with world-class breaks at **Woolamai**, **Smiths Beach**, **Summerand Beach** and **Cat Bay**. And just to prove that there's something for everyone, Phillip Island has its **Motorcycle Grand Prix racing circuit** and attached History of Motorsport Museum.

✖️ 🛏️ p92

The Drive » Leave the island via the causeway at Newhaven, then cruise along the pancake-flat B460 through Wonthaggi and

Bass Strait

on to Inverloch just 50km from where your day's journey began.

----

② Inverloch

Inverloch is just far enough off main roads to feel like a secret – most visitors to Phillip Island are day-trippers who never make it this far, while those heading for the Prom cross Gippsland further north. And at the heart of this secret locals like to keep to themselves are fabulous surf, calm inlet beaches and outstanding diving and snorkelling; try **Offshore Surf School** (📞0407 374 743; www.offshoresurfschool.com.au; 32 Park St; 2hr lesson $60) if you feel inspired to learn how to catch a wave. Add in an eclectic place to stay and some good eating options and you, too, will soon want to keep the secret all to yourself.

The Drive » You could take the quiet and narrow back roads along the coast to Wilsons Prom, but we prefer to zip northeast from Inverloch along the B460 for 10km before taking the turn-off to Koonwarra, a further 11km through rolling dairy country away to the northeast.

----

③ Koonwarra (p93)

Blink and you could very easily miss Koonwarra, tucked away as it is in verdant country along the South Gippsland Hwy. But this is one tiny township worth seeking out, having built itself a reputation

as something of a niche foodie destination. Much of the appeal centres on two places. The first is the **Koonwarra Food & Wine Store** (📞03-5664 2285; www.koonwarrastore.com; cnr South Gippsland Hwy & Koala Dr; mains $12-26; ⏰8.30am-4pm), with its fresh produce and innovative menus in a gorgeous garden setting. Also worth lingering over is **Milly & Romeo's Artisan Bakery & Cooking School** (📞03-5664 2211; www.millyandromeos.com.au; 1 Koala Dr; adult/child from $90/50; ⏰9.30am-4.30pm Thu & Fri, 8.30am-4.30pm Sat & Sun, longer hours in summer), Victoria's first organic-certified cooking school, which offers short courses in making cakes, bread, traditional pastries, French classics and pasta, as well as running cooking classes for kids. But wait, there's more. If you happen upon Koonwarra on the first Saturday morning of the month, there'll be the **Farmers Market** (📞0408 619 182; www.kfm.org.au; Memorial Park, Koala Dr;

LINK YOUR TRIP

3 Mornington Peninsula

The road from Phillip Island to Red Hill (127km) connects you to the end point of the trip around the Mornington Peninsula.

⏱8am-1pm 1st Sat of month) with organic everything (fruit, vegetables, berries, coffee), plus hormone-free beef and chemical-free cheeses. There's even a nearby winery where you can rest your head for the night...

✕ 🛏 p93

The Drive » From Koonwarra, the C444 sweeps down through Meeniyan, artsy Fish Creek and Yanakie, bound for the Prom. The further you go the wilder the land becomes, and the dramatic forested outcrops of the Prom's headlands soon come into view. When you reach the national park, slow down and watch for wildlife and, at regular intervals, fine little trails down to wonderful beaches.

- - - - - - - - - -

TRIP HIGHLIGHT

❹ Wilsons Promontory National Park (p94)

The southernmost tip of mainland Australia, Wilsons Promontory (or 'The Prom' to its many friends) is a wild and wonderful place. Its dense woodland shelters a rich portfolio of native Australian wildlife and its combination of stirring coastal scenery and secluded white-sand beaches have made it one of the most popular national parks in Australia. The **Lilly Pilly Gully Nature Walk** (5km), **Mt Oberon Summit** (7km) and **Squeaky Beach Nature Walk** (5km) will give you a chance to stretch your legs and get a taste of the Prom's appeal.

DETOUR: BUNURONG MARINE & COASTAL PARK

Start: ❷ Inverloch

The inland route to Inverloch may be singularly lacking in drama, but the same can't be said for the 13km detour southwest to Cape Paterson. This stunning cliff-hugging drive looks out upon the **Bunurong Marine & Coastal Park**, and this surprising little park offers some of Australia's best snorkelling and diving – contact **SEAL Diving Services** (p92) to line up gear and guides. If you're going it alone and have the equipment to hand, **Eagles Nest**, **Shack Bay**, the **Caves** and **Twin Reefs** are great for snorkelling. **The Oaks** is the locals' favourite surf beach. The Caves took the archaeological world by storm in the early 1990s when dinosaur remains dating back 120 million years were discovered here; digs are still underway at the site.

- - - - - - - - - -

Even if you don't stray beyond Tidal River (where there's no fuel to be had), you'll catch a sense of the Prom's magic, with car-park access off the Tidal River road leading to gorgeous beaches and lookouts and with tame wildlife everywhere. Swimming is safe at the stunning beaches at **Norman Bay** (Tidal River) and around the headland at **Squeaky Beach** – the ultra-fine quartz sand here really does squeak beneath your feet!

✕ 🛏 p96

The Drive » Retrace your route northwest back up the C444 for 45km, then turn northeast towards Foster (a further 14km). From Foster, it's 48km to Port Albert along the A440, with a signed turn-off 5km before the town. En route, there are fine Prom views away to the south.

❺ Port Albert

Port Albert looks out over the water to a number of islands and has developed a reputation as a trendy stopover for boating, fishing and sampling the local seafood that's been a mainstay of this place for more than 150 years. The town proudly pronounces itself Gippsland's first established port, and many of the historic timber buildings in the main street were built in the 1850s and bear a brass plaque, detailing their age and previous use.

The Drive » Return to the A440, pass through Yarram, then wind down the window and breathe in the salty sea air. Around 64km from Yarram, take the C496 turn-off southeast to Seaspray (27km).

Tidal River (p94)

DETOUR:
AUSTRALIAN ALPS
WALKING TRACK

One of Australia's best and most challenging walks, the Australian Alps Walking Trail begins in Walhalla and ends near Canberra. This 655km epic traverses the valleys and ridge lines of Victoria's High Country, and en route to Tharwa in the Australian Capital Territory (ACT) it climbs to the summit of Mt Bogong, Mt Kosciuszko and Bimberi Peak, the highest points in Victoria, New South Wales and the ACT respectively. Making the full trek is a serious undertaking that requires good navigational skills and high levels of fitness and self-sufficiency. If you're planning on doing the walk, which takes up to eight weeks to complete, track down a copy of *Australian Alps Walking Track* by John and Monica Chapman.

TRIP HIGHLIGHT

6 Ninety Mile Beach

Quiet little Seaspray, a low-key, low-rise seaside village of prefab houses, feels stuck in a 1950s time warp, but the town itself plays second fiddle to what stretches out from its doorstep. To paraphrase the immortal words of Crocodile Dundee...that's not a beach, *this* is a beach. Isolated Ninety Mile Beach is a narrow strip of sand backed by dunes, featuring lagoons and stretching unbroken for more or less 90 miles (150km) from near McLoughlins Beach to the channel at Lakes

Entrance. Standing on the sand and watching the beach unfurl to the northeast while waves curl and crash along its length you'll likely be silenced by the vast emptiness and sheer beauty of it all.

The Drive » With a last, longing look over your shoulder, steel yourself for the least interesting stretch of journey, the 127km to Walhalla that goes something like this: take the C496 for 27km, then the A440 for 6km into Sale. From there it's 55 downright dull kilometres to Traralgon, before the final 34km through rich forest to Walhalla.

TRIP HIGHLIGHT

7 Walhalla (p97)

Welcome to Victoria's best-preserved and most charming historic town.

Tiny Walhalla lies hidden high in the green hills and forests of west Gippsland. It's a postcard-pretty collection of sepia-toned period cottages and other timber buildings (some original, most reconstructed). The setting, too, is gorgeous, strung out along a deep, forested valley with Stringers Creek running through the centre of the township. In its gold-mining heyday in the 1860s, Walhalla's population was 5000. It fell to just 10 people in 1998 (when mains electricity arrived in the town). Like all great ghost towns, the dead that are buried in the stunningly sited cemetery vastly outnumber the living. The best way to see the town is on foot – take the tramline walk (45 minutes), which begins from opposite the general store soon after you enter town. A tour of the **Long Tunnel Extended Gold Mine** (p98) offers insights into why Walhalla existed at all, while the **Walhalla Goldfields Railway** (p98) is a fine adjunct to your visit, snaking as it does along Stringers Creek Gorge, passing lovely forested gorge country and crossing a number of trestle bridges en route.

✗ ⌂ p98

Homestead, Walhalla

Mornington Peninsula

3

The Mornington Peninsula, southeast of Melbourne, is one of the city's favourite summer playgrounds, with exceptional beaches all along the shoreline and wonderful wineries in the interior.

TRIP HIGHLIGHTS

29 km

Sorrento
Sophisticated resort town where the livin's good

146 km

Red Hill
Wineries and other foodie finds with bay views nearby

START
Mornington

Portsea
Surf
Beach

2

Dromana

Rosebud
Blairgowrie

Mornington
Peninsula
National Park

Arthurs
Seat
(305m)

7

FINISH

**Stony
Point**

Tankerton

Gunnamatta Beach

4

**Cape
Schanck**

Cape Schanck
Lighthouse

**Mornington Peninsula
National Park**
Dramatic coastal scenery, wild beaches and splendid lighthouse views

40 km

**3–4 DAYS
146KM /
91 MILES**

GREAT FOR...

BEST TIME TO GO

October to March; winter months can be cold and the towns empty.

**ESSENTIAL
PHOTO**

The view from Cape Schanck Lighthouse.

**BEST FOR
OUTDOORS**

Swim with the dolphins off Sorrento then head for Portsea Back Beach.

Left Boardwalk, Cape Schanck (p104)

Mornington Peninsula

To fully appreciate Melbourne's privileged bayside location, take the long drive south to where the bay meets the ocean, passing en route the lovely seaside towns of Mornington, Sorrento and Portsea. This fairly sedate coastline takes on a whole new personality in the wave-lashed Mornington Peninsula National Park, while Flinders is a quietly beautiful place. Finally, the area around Red Hill is one of Victoria's most important and pleasureable wine areas.

❶ Mornington (p99)

Pretty Mornington, with its cute bathing boxes and swimming beaches, is the gateway to the peninsula's holiday coastal strip – just beyond the reaches of Melbourne's urban sprawl. Originally part of the lands of the Boonwurrung people, it was founded as a European township in 1854. Echoes of those days remain. Grand old buildings around Main St include the 1892 **Grand Hotel**, the 1860

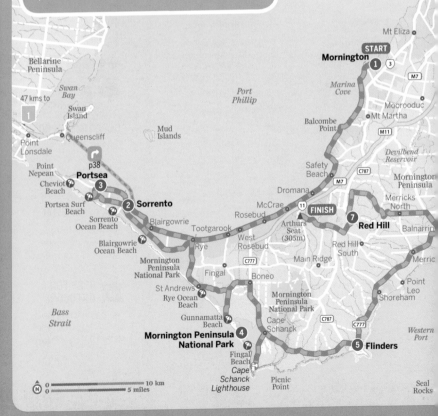

Old Court House, on the corner of Main St and the Esplanade, and the 1862 **Police Lock-Up** behind it. On the opposite corner is the 1863 **post office building**. For views over the harbour, take a walk along the 1850s **pier** and around the **Schnapper Point** foreshore boardwalk past the **Matthew Flinders monument** that commemorates his 1802 landing. **Mothers Beach** is the main swimming beach, while at **Fossil Beach** there are remains of a lime-burning kiln; fossils found here date back 25 million years! And it's at **Mills Beach** where you can see the colourful and photogenic bathing boxes.

✗ ⚐ p100

The Drive » From Mornington, the Esplanade heads south for the gorgeous scenic drive towards Sorrento, skirting the rocky Port Phillip Bay foreshore. Inland, the Nepean Hwy (B110) takes a less-scenic route and again becomes the Mornington Peninsula Fwy.

- - - - - - - - - - - -

TRIP HIGHLIGHT

② Sorrento (p100)

Historic Sorrento, the site of Victoria's first official European settlement in 1803, is the standout town on the Mornington Peninsula. The town has so much going for it – beautiful limestone buildings, ocean and bay beaches, and a buzzing seaside summer atmosphere – that it should come as no surprise that it has become one of Victoria's most refined resort towns. Twas ever thus here – some of the grandest old buildings, among them the **Sorrento Hotel** (1871), **Continental Hotel** (1875) and **Koonya Hotel** (1878), were built to serve well-to-do 19th-century visitors from Melbourne. These days, Sorrento also boasts some of the best cafes and restaurants on the peninsula, and the main street is lined with galleries, boutiques, and craft and antique shops. And on no account miss the chance to go swimming with dolphins with **Polperro Dolphin Swims** (☎03-5988 8437; www.polperro.com.au; adult/child sightseeing $55/35, dolphin & seal swimming adult & child $135) or **Moonraker Charters** (☎03-5984 4211; www.moonrakercharters.com.au; 7 George St, Sorrento; adult/child sightseeing $55/44, dolphin & seal swimming $129/115).

✗ ⚐ p101

LINK YOUR TRIP

1 Great Ocean Road

Head north from Mornington or Red Hill to Melbourne, skip across town and down the A1, bypassing Geelong en route to Torquay. Alternatively, take the ferry from Sorrento to Queescliff, from where it is a short drive to Torquay.

2 Gippsland & Wilsons Promontory

Phillip Island is a natural bedfellow for the Mornington Peninsula; take the back road to Koo Wee Rup and down to the island (127km).

Bathing boxes near Portsea (p103)

The Drive » The 4km hop from Sorrento to Portsea follows the coast – watch for fine bays views on the Portsea approach.

- - - - - - - - - - - -

DETOUR: QUEENSCLIFF

Start: ❷ Sorrento

Historic Queenscliff, across the water from Sorrento on the Bellarine Peninsula, is one of coastal Victoria's lovelist towns. It's a place of heritage streetscapes, the formidable **Fort Queenscliff** (☎03-5258 1488, for midweek tours 0403 193 311; www.fortqueenscliff.com. au; cnr Gellibrand & King Sts; adult/child/family $10/5/25; ⊙1pm & 3pm Sat & Sun, daily school holidays), fine cafes and restaurants, and parkland sweeping down to the beach. From some areas, particularly from the lookout at the southern end of Hesse St (next to the bowling club), the views across the Port Phillip Heads and Bass Strait are glorious. And getting here couldn't be easier – the **Queenscliff–Sorrento Ferry** (☎03-5258 3244; www.searoad.com.au; one way foot passenger adult/child $11/8, 2 adults & car $73; ⊙hourly 7am-6pm) crosses the bay in 40 minutes throughout the day.

❸ Portsea (p103)

If you thought Sorrento was classy, wait until you see Portsea. The last village on the peninsula, wee Portsea is where many of Melbourne's wealthiest families have built seaside mansions. You can walk the **Farnsworth Track** (1.5km, 30 minutes) out to scenic London Bridge, a natural rock formation, and spot middens of the Boonwurrung people who once called this area home. Diving and snorkelling are both possible through **Dive Victoria** (☎03-5984 3155; www.divevictoria.com.au; 3752 Point Nepean Rd; snorkelling $85, s/d dive with gear $130/210), while **Portsea Surf Beach** is where the ocean's sheer power never fails to impress. Back in town, Portsea's pulse is the iconic, sprawling, half-timber **Portsea Hotel**, an enormous pub with a great lawn and terrace area looking out over the bay.

✗ ⊨ p103

The Drive » Your next destination, Mornington Peninsula National Park, actually extends into the Portsea hinterland, and there are numerous access points – Portsea Surf Beach, along the back road between Portsea and Rye, at Gunnamatta Beach and, perhaps most memorably, at Cape Schanck.

TRIP HIGHLIGHT

❹ Mornington Peninsula National Park (p103)

Stretching from Portsea on the sliver of coastline to Cape Schanck and inland to the Greens Bush area, this national park showcases the peninsula's most beautiful and rugged ocean beaches. Along here are the cliffs, bluffs and crashing surf beaches of Portsea, Sorrento, Blairgowrie, Rye, St Andrews, Gunnamatta and Cape Schanck; swimming and surfing are dangerous at these beaches, so swim only between the flags at Gunnamatta and Portsea during summer. Built in 1859, Cape Schanck Light

house (p104) is a photogenic working lighthouse; from the lighthouse, descend the steps of the boardwalk that leads to the craggy cape for outstanding views. Longer walks are also possible.

⊨ p104

The Drive » From Cape Schanck Lighthouse, return to the C777 and follow it for 11km east along the coast to Flinders. Watch for sweeping ocean views, especially in the middle section of the route.

❺ Flinders (p104)

Little Flinders, where the thrashing ocean beaches give way to Western Port Bay, has so far been largely spared the development of the Port Phillip Bay towns. As a consequence, Flinders remains a

Vineyards (p103), Red Hill

Pier, Flinders (p104)

delightful little community and is still home to a busy fishing fleet. Surfers have been coming to Flinders for decades, drawn by ocean-side breaks such as Gunnery, Big Left and Cyril's, and golfers know the clifftop **Flinders Golf Club** (p102) course as the most scenic and wind blown in Victoria. The historic **Flinders Hotel** (p104) has been a beacon on this sleepy street corner longer than anyone can remember. It's not that there's a lot to do here. It's more about sampling the Mornington Peninsula as it used to be before the crowds began arriving en masse.

🍴 🛏 p104

The Drive >> Follow the C777 along the Westernport Bay coast northeast to Balnarring. After a further 7km, turn off southeast to Stony Point (7km from the turn-off). Leave your car and take the ferry from Stony Point to French Island's Tankerton Jetty.

6 French Island (p104)

Exposed, windswept and wonderfully isolated, French Island is two-thirds national park and

retains a real sense of tranquility – you can only get here by passenger ferry, so it's virtually traffic-free, and there's no mains water or electricity! The main attractions are bushwalking and cycling, taking in wetlands, checking out one of Australia's largest koala colonies and observing a huge variety of birds. Pick up the Parks Victoria brochure at the Tankerton Jetty for a list of walks and cycling routes. All roads on the island are unsealed and some are quite sandy. From the jetty it's around 2km to the licensed **French Island General Store** (📞03-5980 1209; Tankerton Rd, Lot 1; bike hire $25; ⏰8am-6pm, from 9am Sun), which also serves as post office, tourist information and bike-hire centre.

The Drive >> Take the ferry back to Stony Point, return the 13km to Balnarring, then cut inland via Merricks North to Red Hill.

TRIP HIGHLIGHT

7 Red Hill

The undulating hills of the peninsula's interior around Red Hill and

Main Ridge is a lovely region of trees, where you can spend a sublime afternoon hopping around winery cellar doors and restaurants. It can be difficult to choose (and pity the poor designated driver who'll be unable to drink), but we'd visit **Red Hill Brewery** (📞03-5989 2959; www.redhillbrewery. com.au; 88 Shoreham Rd; ⏰11am-6pm long weekends and by appointment), **Port Phillip Estate** (p103) and **Ten Minutes by Tractor** (p103). If you happen upon Red Hill on the first Saturday of the month (except in winter), the **Red Hill Market** (www.craftmarkets.com. au; ⏰8am-1pm 1st Sat of month Sep-May) is well worth the effort. Whenever you're here, allow time to pick your own strawberries at **Sunny Ridge Strawberry Farm** (📞03-5989 4500; www. sunnyridge.com.au; cnr Shands & Mornington-Flinders Rds; adult/child $8/4; ⏰9am-5pm Nov-Apr, 11am-4pm Sat & Sun May-Oct) and take the 16km round-trip detour to **Arthurs Seat**, which, at 305m, is the highest point on the Port Phillip Bay coast. It's the ideal place to take it all in and contemplate just how far you've come.

Goldfields & Macedon

4

Gold was what made Victoria great, and this lovely meander through old gold-mining towns and rolling hill country is one of the state's more agreeable and lesser-known drives.

TRIP HIGHLIGHTS

160 km

Clunes
Impeccable gold heritage and fabulous books

Bendigo ●

81 km

Maldon
Storybook mining village, perfectly preserved

5

B180   C282   Chewton

Newstead

Malmsbury

7

Daylesford ●

2

● Macedon
START

8 FINISH

Ballarat
Victoria's premier gold-mining town

201 km

Woodend & Hanging Rock
Iconic volcanic outcrop swirling with mystery

7 km

4–5 DAYS
201KM / 125 MILES

GREAT FOR...

BEST TIME TO GO

Southern areas can be bitterly cold in winter. Autumn is wonderful around the Macedon Ranges.

ESSENTIAL PHOTO

Maldon's main street.

BEST FOR HISTORY

Castlemaine has fabulous gold-rush architecture and a palpable sense of history.

Left Mt Macedon (p44)

4

Goldfields & Macedon

The Macedon Ranges are the perfect place to begin, home as it is to haunting Hanging Rock and some lovely little towns that capture the essence of rural Victoria. From then on, it's stately, historic gold-mining towns all the way to Ballarat, which wears the region's gold-mining heritage like a glittering badge of honour. En route, stop by pretty little Kyneton, buzzing Castlemaine, timeworn Maryborough and Victoria's permier booktown, Clunes.

1 Macedon

Less than an hour northwest of Melbourne and yet a world away, Macedon is a quiet unassuming town. It may lack the historical streetscapes of other towns along the route, but its green parklands serve as an agreeable prelude to the Macedon Ranges, a beautiful area of low mountains, native forest, excellent regional produce and wineries. Charming at any time of the year, these hills can be enveloped in suggestive clouds in winter, but are at their best when bathed in golden autumnal shades. The scenic drive up **Mt Macedon**, a 1010m-high extinct volcano, passes grand mansions and gardens, taking you to picnic areas, walking trails, sweeping lookouts and the huge memorial cross near the summit car park. If you're keen to linger, there are some great wineries (www.macedon rangeswineries.com.au) in the area, while **Wine Tours Victoria** (☎1800 946 386; www.winetours.com.au) can arrange day tours.

The Drive » It's only 7km from Macedon north to Woodend, but forsake the M79 Calder Freeway and take the quieter back road that runs parallel.

LINK YOUR TRIP

1 Great Ocean Road

One of Australia's great road trips begins in Torquay. From Ballarat, drive south on the A300 to the Geelong bypass, where it is roughly 30km to Torquay.

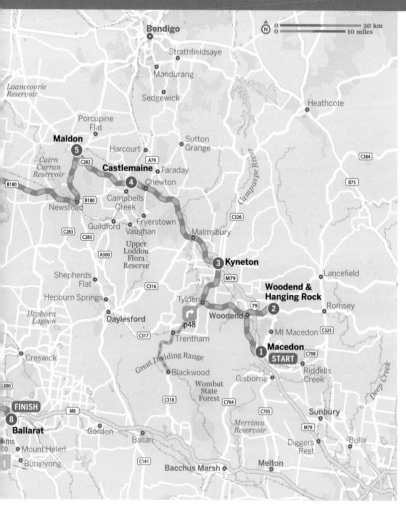

p48

p106

TRIP HIGHLIGHT

2 Woodend & Hanging Rock (p106)

Pleasant little Woodend has a certain bucolic appeal – the wide streets, the free-standing clock-tower, the smattering of heritage buildings with wide verandahs and wrought-ironwork. But it's the setting here that truly beguiles, amid rolling hills and expansive woodlands latticed by vineyards. East of town lies **Hanging Rock** (www. visitmacedonranges.com; per vehicle $10; ⏰ 9am-5pm), an ancient and captivating place made famous by the unsettling Joan Lindsay novel (and subsequent film by Peter Weir) *Picnic at Hanging Rock*. The volcanic rock formations are the sacred site of the traditional owners, the Wurundjeri people. They also once served as a hideout for bushrangers, and many mysteries and legends surround it; an eerie energy is said to be felt by many who climb among the boulders. From the summit, a 20-minute climb, splendid views of Mt Macedon and beyond open up. Spreading out below the rock is its famous racecourse, which hosts two excellent picnic race meetings on New Year's Day and Australia Day, and kangaroos the rest of the time.

✕ 🛏 p106

The Drive » From Woodend, head west 12km to Tylden, from where the road branches southwest to your Trentham-Blackwood detour, or north to Kyneton. Whichever you choose, it's a pretty drive through sweeping farmlands and light eucalyptus woodlands.

- - - - - - - - - -

③ Kyneton (p107)

Kyneton's existence predates the gold rush by a year, and it's the first of the gold-mining towns you come to on this trip. It was the main coach stop between Melbourne and Bendigo, and the centre for the farmers who supplied the diggings with fresh produce. These days, Kyneton serves a similar purpose as a regional centre set amid prosperous farming country, and it's filled with the kind of attractions that are a staple of the gold-era towns, but it's a whole lot quieter, too often overlooked on the rush to the regional centres of Daylesford, Bendigo or Castlemaine.

Piper St is a historic precinct lined with bluestone buildings that have been transformed into cafes, antique shops, museums and restaurants. If you're keen to see what many of these buildings looked like on the inside, try the **Kyneton Historical Museum** (☏03-5422 1228; 67 Piper St; adult/child $6.50/3; ☺11am-4pm Fri-Sun), decked out in period furnishings, while the **Botanic Gardens** (Clowes St) is a lovely spot beside the Campaspe River.

✕ 🛏 p107

The Drive » The well-worn trail from Melbourne to Castlemaine passes right by Kyneton, but we recommend taking the quieter parallel roads that shadow the Calder Fwy. That way you'll get to see Malmsbury and lovely little Chewton on your way into Castlemaine.

- - - - - - - - - -

④ Castlemaine (p107)

In the heart of the central Victorian goldfields, Castlemaine is one of the most happening places in Victoria, where a growing community of artists and tree-changers live amid some inspiring architecture and gardens. It all stems from the mid-19th century when Castlemaine was *the* thriving marketplace for the goldfields. Even after the gold rush subsided, Castlemaine built a

MAGSPACE/SHUTTERSTOCK ©

reputation for industry and innovation – this was the birthplace of the Castlemaine XXXX beer-brewing company (now based in Queensland). Historic buildings littered around town include the Roman basilica facade of the old **Castlemaine Market** (1862) on Mostyn St; the **Theatre Royal** (1856) on Hargreaves St; the **post office** (1894); and the original **courthouse building** (1851) on Goldsmith Cres. For a good view over town, head up to the **Burke & Wills Monument** on

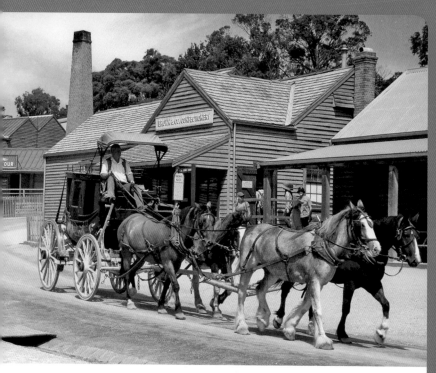

Sovereign Hill (p111)

Wills St (follow Lyttleton St east of the centre). And to see why the buzz around Castlemaine never abates, stop by for a beer at the **Bridge Hotel** (☎03-5472 1161; http://bridgehotelcastlemaine. com; 21 Walker St; ⏰4-11pm Mon-Wed, to 1am Thu, to 1pm Fri, noon-midnight Sat, to 11pm Sun), one of regional Victoria's best live-music venues.

✖️ 🛏️ p108

The Drive » The C282 from Castlemaine to Maldon (16km) passes through the box-ironbark forests of Victoria's gold country. It's a lovely drive to a lovely place.

TRIP HIGHLIGHT

❺ Maldon (p109)

Like a pop-up folk museum, the whole of tiny Maldon is a well-preserved relic of the gold-rush era, with many fine buildings constructed from local stone. The population is significantly lower than the 20,000 who used to work the local goldfields, but this is still a living, working town – packed with tourists on week-ends but reverting to its sleepy self during the week. Evidence of those

heady mining days can be seen around town – you can't miss the 24m-high **Beehive Chimney**, just east of Main St, while the **Old Post Office** (p110), built in 1870, was the childhood home of local author Henry Handel Richardson. A short trip south along High St reveals the remains of the **North British Mine**, once one of the world's richest mines.

✖️ 🛏️ p110

The Drive » On the way out of town, don't miss the 3km drive up to Mt Tarrengower for panoramic views from the poppet-head lookout. Once

47

DETOUR: TRENTHAM & BLACKWOOD

Start ❷ Woodend

The small historic township of **Trentham** (pop 630) sits at the top of the Great Dividing Range, midway between Woodend and Daylesford. At an elevation of 700m it's noticeably cooler than the surrounding areas, and is worth a visit to stroll its quaint streetscape with some excellent eateries. Although it's growing in popularity, visit on a weekday and you're likely to have the place all to yourself.

A mere 16km away to the south and surrounded by state forest, tiny **Blackwood** is a lesser-known, even-smaller version of the Trentham charm. On the main strip is **Blackwood Merchant**, a cafe-general store with local produce and wines. Its back patio has lovely forest views. On the corner is the historic **Blackwood Hotel** (☏ 03-5368 6501; www.blackwoodpub.com; Martin St; r $90), established in 1868 with plenty of atmposhere, pub meals and basic accommodation. There's also the quaint **Garden of St Erth** (☏ 03-5368 6514; www.diggers.com.au/gardens-cafes/gardens/st-erth.aspx; Simmons Reef Rd, Blackwood; entry $10; ☉ garden 9am-5pm, cafe 10am-4pm Thu-Mon), a garden nursery that's centered around an 1860 sandstone cottage with a cafe serving produce grown onsite.

you're ready to leave, head due south towards Newstead, then west along the B180 through Joyces Creek and Carisbrook to Maryborough.

❻ Maryborough (p110)

Maryborough is an essential part of central Victoria's 'Golden Triangle' experience, but it's sufficiently far west to miss out on the day-trippers that flock to Castlemaine and Maldon. Those that do make it this far are rewarded with some splendid Victorian-era buildings, but **Maryborough Railway Station** (☏ 03-5461 4683; 38 Victoria St; ☉ 10am-5pm) leaves them all for dead. Built in 1892 the inordinately large station, complete with clock tower, was described by Mark Twain as 'a train station with a town attached'. Today it houses a mammoth antique emporium, a regional wine centre and a cafe. Prospectors still turn up a nugget or two in the Maryborough area. If you're interested in finding your own gold nuggets, **Coiltek Gold Centre** (☏ 03-5460 4700; www.maryboroughgoldcentre.com.au; 6 Drive-in Ct; ☉ 9am-5pm) offers full-day prospecting courses with state-of-the-art metal detectors. It also sells and hires out prospecting gear.

✕ 🛏 p110

The Drive ›› The C287 runs south and then southeast for 32km to Clunes. It's an attractive, quiet road with stands of forest interspersed with open farmlands; watch for Mt Beckworth rising away to the southwest as you near Clunes.

TRIP HIGHLIGHT

❼ Clunes

Clunes may be small, but this is where it all began. It was here, roughly halfway between Maryborough and Ballarat, that a find in June 1851 sparked the gold rush that would transform Victoria's fortunes. These days, the small town is a quintessential gold-mining relic, with gorgeous 19th-century porticoed buildings whose grandeur seems way out of proportion to the town's current size. But Clunes has another claim to fame. The town hosts the annual **Booktown Book Fair** (www.clunesbooktown.com.au) in early May and is home to no fewer than (at last count) seven bookstores, with a focus on the secondhand trade.

The Drive ≫ There are two possible routes to Ballarat, although we prefer the quieter C287. All along its 24km, there's an growing sense of accumulating clamour as the flat yellow farmlands south of Clunes yield to the outskirts of Ballarat as you pass over the Western Hwy.

TRIP HIGHLIGHT

⑧ Ballarat (p111)

Ballarat is one of the greatest gold-mining towns on earth, a thriving testament to a mineral that continues to provide most of the town's major attractions, even long after the gold rush ended. Partly that heritage survives in the grand buildings scattered regally around the city centre. Take the time to walk along Lydiard St in particular, one of Australia's finest streetscapes for Victorian-era architecture. Impressive buildings include **Her Majesty's Theatre**, **Craig's Royal Hotel**, **George Hotel** and the **Art Gallery** (☎03-5320 5858; www.balgal.com; 40 Lydiard St Nth; ⏰10am-5pm), which also houses a wonderful collection of early colonial paintings with works from noted Australian artists. But Ballarat's fine story is most stirringly told in two museums that hark back to the town's glory days: the fabulous, re-created gold-mining village at **Sovereign Hill** (p111) and the stunning new **Museum of Australian Democracy at Eureka** (p113).

✕ 🛏 p114

Maryborough Railway Station

Destinations

Melbourne (p52)

Stylish, arty Melbourne is a city that's both dynamic and cosmopolitan, and proud of its place as Australia's cultural capital.

Great Ocean Road (p79)

The most iconic of Australian road trips takes in world-class surf breaks, ancient rainforests and koala-filled tree canopies.

Gippsland (p90)

Here you will find some of the state's most absorbing, unspoilt and beautiful wilderness areas and beaches.

Mornington Peninsula (p99)

Melbourne's summer playground since the 1870s, the peninsula has fine beaches and some of the state's best food and wine.

Goldfields (p106)

History, nature and culture combine spectacularly in Victoria's regional heart.

Gentle hills of Gippsland
AUSTRALIAN SCENICS/GETTY IMAGES ©

Melbourne

Melbourne regularly ranks as one of the world's most liveable cities, and it's not hard to see why – as the epicurean, sporting and, arguably, culture capital of Australia, there is much to see and do.

MELBOURNE

POP 4.25 MILLION

Melbourne is best experienced as a local would: dive into the city's lanes or climb to an open-air bar atop a former industrial building, and you'll very quickly learn why Melbourne is Australia's most happening city.

◉ Sights

◉ Central Melbourne

Melbourne's wide main streets and legion of lanes buzz day and night, seven days a week with museums and art galleries dotted throughout. There are two big ends of town: skyscrapers cluster on the east and west ends of the grid – these areas are mostly used by business. Southern Cross Station sits to the west, with Docklands Stadium and the regenerated Docklands beyond. Opposite the central Flinders Street Station, Federation Sq (better known as Fed Square) squats beside the Yarra River and has become a favourite Melbourne gathering place. To the east is the top ('Paris') end of town, with its monumental gold-rush-era buildings and designer stores.

★**Federation Square**   SQUARE
(Map p58; www.fedsquare.com.au; cnr Flinders & Swanston Sts; 🚋1, 3, 5, 6, 8, 16, 64, 67, 72, 🚆Flinders St) It took some time, but Melburnians have embraced Federation Sq, accepting it as the congregation place it was meant to be – somewhere to celebrate, protest, watch major sporting events or just hang out. Occupying a prominent city block, Fed Square is far from square: its undulating and patterned forecourt is paved with 460,000 hand-laid cobblestones from the Kimberley region; while its buildings are clad in a fractal-patterned reptilian skin. Highly recommended free tours of Fed Square depart Monday to Saturday at 11am; spaces are limited, so get here 10 to 15 minutes early. The square has free wi-fi, and there's free daily tai chi from 7.30am and meditation at 12.30pm on Tuesday.

★**Ian Potter Centre:**
NGV Australia   GALLERY
(Map p58; 🎧03-8620 2222; www.ngv.vic.gov.au; Federation Sq; exhibition costs vary; ⊘10am-5pm Tue-Sun; 🚋1, 3, 5, 6, 8, 16, 64, 67, 72, 🚆Flinders St) Hidden away in the basement of Federation Sq, the Ian Potter Centre is the second half of the National Gallery of Victoria (NGV), set up to showcase the gallery's impressive collection of Australian works. Set over three levels, it's a mix of permanent (free) and temporary (ticketed) exhibitions, comprising paintings, decorative arts, photography, prints, sculpture and fashion. There's also a great museum gift shop. Free tours are conducted daily at 11am, noon, 1pm and 2pm. The permanent Aboriginal exhibition on the ground floor is stunning, and seeks to challenge ideas of the 'authentic'.

There are some particularly fine examples of Papunya painting and interesting use of mediums from bark and didgeridoos to contemporary sculpture and dot paintings on canvas.

Australian Centre for the Moving Image
MUSEUM

(ACMI; Map p58; ☑03-8663 2200; www.acmi.net.au; Federation Sq; ⊙10am-6pm; 🚋1, 3, 5, 6, 8, 16, 64, 67, 72, 🚇Flinders St) **FREE** Managing to educate, enthral and entertain in equal parts, ACMI is a visual feast that pays homage to Australian cinema and TV, offering an insight into the modern-day Australian psyche. Its floating screens don't discriminate against age, with TV shows, games and movies on call, making it a great place to waste a day watching TV and not feel guilty about it. Free tours are conducted daily at 11am and 2.30pm.

★Birrarung Marr
PARK

(Map p58; btwn Federation Sq & the Yarra River; 🚋1, 3, 5, 6, 8, 16, 64, 67, 72, 🚇Flinders St) The three-terraced Birrarung Marr is a welcome addition to Melbourne's patchwork of parks and gardens, featuring grassy knolls, river promenades, a thoughtful planting of indigenous flora and great views of the city and the river. There's also a scenic walking route to the Melbourne Cricket Ground (p61) via the 'talking' William Barak Bridge – listen out for songs, words and sounds representing Melbourne's cultural diversity as you walk.

★Hosier Lane
STREET

(Map p58; Hosier Lane; 🚋75, 70) Melbourne's most celebrated lane for street art, Hosier Lane's cobbled length draws camera-wielding crowds snapping edgy graffiti, stencils and art installations. Subject matter runs mostly to the political and counter cultural, spiced with irreverent humour. Pieces change almost daily (not even a Banksy is safe here). Be sure to see Rutledge Lane (which horseshoes around Hosier), too.

Flinders Street Station
HISTORIC BUILDING

(Map p58; cnr Flinders & Swanston Sts) If ever there was a true symbol of the city, Flinders Street Station would have to be it. Built in 1854, it was Melbourne's first railway station, and you'd be hard pressed to find a Melburnian who hasn't uttered the phrase 'Meet me under the clocks' at one time or another (the popular rendezvous spot is located at the station's front entrance). Stretching along the Yarra, it's a beautiful neoclassical building topped with a striking octagonal dome.

St Paul's Cathedral
CHURCH

(Map p58; ☑03-9653 4333; www.stpaulscathedral.org.au; cnr Flinders & Swanston Sts; ⊙8am-6pm Sun-Fri, to 5pm Sat) Opposite Federation Sq stands the magnificent Anglican St Paul's Cathedral. Services were celebrated on this site from the city's first days. Built between 1880 and 1891, the present church is the work of distinguished ecclesiastical architect William Butterfield (a case of architecture by proxy, as he did not condescend to visit Melbourne, instead sending drawings from England). It features ornate stained-glass windows, made between 1887 and 1890, and holds excellent music programs.

Old Treasury Building
MUSEUM

(Map p58; ☑03-9651 2233; www.oldtreasurybuilding.org.au; Spring St; ⊙10am-4pm, closed Sat; 🚋112, 🚇Parliament) **FREE** The fine neoclassical architecture of the Old Treasury (c 1862), designed by JJ Clarke, is a telling mix of hubris and functionality. The basement vaults were built to house the millions of pounds worth of loot that came from the Victorian goldfields and now feature multimedia displays telling gold-rush stories. Also downstairs is the charmingly redolent reconstruction of the 1920s caretaker's residence, which beautifully reveals what life in Melbourne was like in the early part of last century.

Parliament House
HISTORIC BUILDING

(Map p58; ☑03-9651 8568; www.parliament.vic.gov.au; Spring St; ⊙tours 9.30am, 10.30am, 11.30am, 1.30pm, 2.30pm & 3.45pm Mon-Fri; 🚋City Circle, 86,

Flinders Street Station

Melbourne

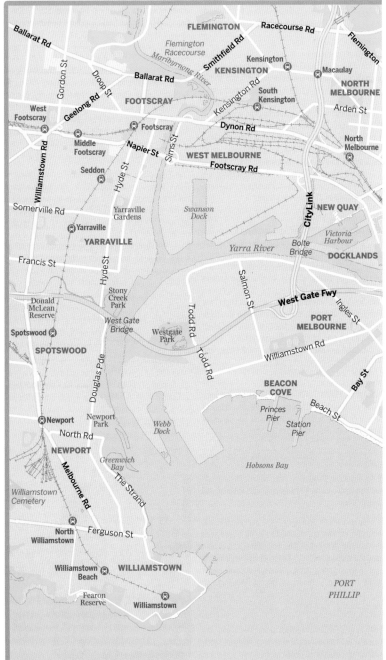

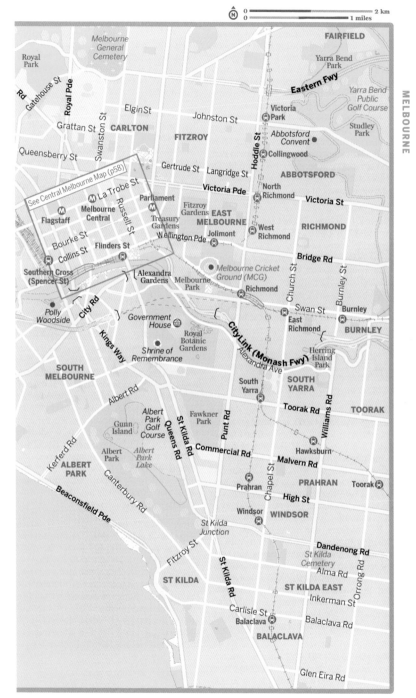

96, ⊠ Parliament) The grand steps of Victoria's parliament (c 1856) are often dotted with slow-moving, tulle-wearing brides smiling for the camera, or placard-holding protesters doing the same. Entry inside is only by tour (free), and you'll see exuberant use of ornamental plasterwork, stencilling and gilt full of gold-rush-era pride and optimism. Building began with the two main chambers: the lower house (now the legislative assembly) and the upper house (now the legislative council).

Australia's first federal parliament sat here from 1901, before moving to Canberra in 1927. Though they've never been used, gun slits are visible just below the roof, and a dungeon is now the cleaners' tearoom.

Chinatown
AREA

(Map p58; Little Bourke St, btwn Spring & Swanston Sts; ⊠ 1, 3, 5, 6, 8, 16, 64, 67, 72) Chinese miners arrived in search of the 'new gold mountain' in the 1850s and settled along this section of Little Bourke St, now flanked by traditional red archways. The Chinese Museum (Map p58; ☑ 03-9662 2888; www.chinesemuseum.com.au; 22 Cohen Pl; adult/child $8/6; ⊙ 10am-5pm) does a wonderful job of putting it into context with five floors of displays, including gold-rush artefacts, dealings under the xenophobic White Australia policy and the stunning 63m-long, 200kg Millennium Dragon that bends around the building – it needs eight people to hold up its head alone.

★ State Library of Victoria
LIBRARY

(Map p58; ☑ 03-8664 7000; www.slv.vic.gov.au; 328 Swanston St; ⊙ 10am-9pm Mon-Thu, to 6pm Fri-Sun; ⊠ 1, 3, 5, 6, 8, 16, 64, 67, 72, ⊠ Melbourne Central) A big player in Melbourne's achievement of being named a Unesco City of Literature in 2008, the State Library has been at the forefront of Melbourne's literary scene since it opened in 1854. With over two million books in its collection, it's a great place to browse.

Its epicentre, the octagonal La Trobe Reading Room, was completed in 1913. Its reinforced-concrete dome was, at the time, the largest of its kind in the world and natural light illuminates its ornate plasterwork and the studious Melbourne writers who come here to pen their works. Another highlight is the collection of Ned Kelly memorabilia, including his suit of armour.

Old Melbourne Gaol
HISTORIC BUILDING

(Map p58; ☑ 03-8663 7228; www.oldmelbourne gaol.com.au; 337 Russell St; adult/child/family $25/13.50/55; ⊙ 9.30am-5pm; ⊠ 24, 30, City

Circle) Built in 1841, this forbidding bluestone prison was in operation until 1929. It's now one of Melbourne's most popular museums, where you can tour the tiny, bleak cells. Around 135 people were hanged here, including Ned Kelly, Australia's most infamous bushranger, in 1880. One of his death masks is on display.

★ Queen Victoria Market
MARKET

(Map p58; www.qvm.com.au; 513 Elizabeth St; ⊙ 6am-2pm Tue & Thu, to 5pm Fri, to 3pm Sat, 9am-4pm Sun; ⊠ Tourist Shuttle, ⊠ 19, 55, 57, 59) With over 600 traders, the Vic Market is the largest open-air market in the southern hemisphere and attracts thousands of shoppers. It's where Melburnians sniff out fresh produce among the booming cries of spruiking fishmongers and fruit-and-veg vendors. The wonderful deli hall (with art deco features) is lined with everything from soft cheeses, wines and Polish sausages to Greek dips, truffle oil and kangaroo biltong.

Koorie Heritage Trust
CULTURAL CENTRE

(Map p58; ☑ 03-8622 2600; www.koorieheritage trust.com; 295 King St; admission by gold coin donation, tours $15; ⊙ 9am-5pm Mon-Fri; ⊠ 24, 30, ⊠ Flagstaff) ⬦ Devoted to southeastern Aboriginal culture, this cultural centre displays interesting artefacts and oral history. Its gallery spaces show a variety of contemporary and traditional work, a model scar tree at the centre's heart, and a permanent chronological display of Victorian Koorie history. Behind the scenes, significant objects are carefully preserved – replicas that can be touched by visitors are used in the displays. The centre is in the process of relocating, so check the website for details. It also runs highly recommended tours to Flagstaff Gardens and along the Yarra, which put the areas into context; call ahead to enquire.

Immigration Museum
MUSEUM

(Map p58; ☑ 13 11 02; www.museumvictoria.com.au/immigrationmuseum; 400 Flinders St; adult/child $12/free; ⊙ 10am-5pm; ⊠ 70, 75) The Immigration Museum uses personal and community voices, images and memorabilia to tell the many stories of Australian immigration. Symbolically housed in the old Customs House, the restored building alone is worth the visit: the Long Room is a magnificent piece of Renaissance Revival architecture.

Sea Life Melbourne Aquarium
AQUARIUM

(Map p58; ☑ 03-9923 5999; www.melbourne aquarium.com.au; cnr Flinders & King Sts; adult/

child/family $38/22/96; ◎9.30am-6pm, last entry 5pm; 🚊70, 75) This aquarium is home to rays, gropers and sharks, all of which cruise around a 2.2-million-litre tank, watched closely by visitors in a see-through tunnel. See the penguins in icy 'Antarctica' or get up close to one of Australia's largest saltwater crocs in the crocodile lair. Divers are thrown to the sharks three times a day; for between $210 and $300 you can join them. Admission tickets are cheaper online.

St Patrick's Cathedral   CHURCH
(◩03-9662 2233; www.stpatrickscathedral.org. au; cnr Gisborne St & Cathedral Pl; ◎9am-5pm Mon-Fri; 🚊112) Head up McArthur St (the extension of Collins St) to see one of the world's largest and finest examples of Gothic Revival architecture. Designed by William Wardell, St Patrick's was named after the patron saint of Ireland, reflecting the local Catholic community's main origin. Construction began in 1863 and continued until spires were added in 1939.

◎ Southbank & Docklands

Southbank, once a gritty industrial site, sits directly across the Yarra from Flinders St. Behind it is the city's major arts precinct. Back down by the river, the promenade stretches to the Crown Casino & Entertainment Complex, a self-proclaimed 'world of entertainment', and further on to South Wharf, the newest development of bars and restaurants. To the city's west lies the Docklands, a mini-city of apartment buildings, offices, restaurants, plazas, public art and parkland.

★NGV International   GALLERY
(◩03-8662 1555; www.ngv.vic.gov.au; 180 St Kilda Rd; exhibition costs vary; ◎10am-5pm Wed-Mon; 🚊Tourist Shuttle, 🚊1, 3, 5, 6, 8, 16, 64, 67, 72) Beyond the water-wall facade you'll find an expansive collection set over three levels, covering international art that runs from the ancient to the contemporary. Key works include a Rembrandt, a Tiepolo and a Bonnard. You might also bump into a Monet, a Modigliani or a Bacon. It's also home to Picasso's *Weeping Woman*, which was the victim of an art heist in 1986. Free 45-minute tours run hourly from 11am to 2pm and alternate to different parts of the collection.

★Arts Centre Melbourne   ARTS CENTRE
(◩bookings 1300 182 183; www.artscentre melbourne.com.au; 100 St Kilda Rd; ◎box office

9am-8.30pm Mon-Fri, 10am-5pm Sat; 🚊Tourist Shuttle, 🚊1, 3, 5, 6, 8, 16, 64, 67, 72, 🚆Flinders St) The Arts Centre is made up of two separate buildings: Hamer Hall (the concert hall) and the theatres building (under the spire). They're linked by a series of landscaped walkways. The George Adams Gallery and St Kilda Road Foyer Gallery are free gallery spaces with changing exhibitions. In the foyer of the theatres building, pick up a self-guided booklet for a tour of art commissioned for the building, including works by Arthur Boyd, Sidney Nolan and Jeffrey Smart.

★Eureka Skydeck   VIEWPOINT
(Map p58; www.eurekaskydeck.com.au; 7 Riverside Quay; adult/child/family $19.50/11/44, The Edge extra $12/8/29; ◎10am-10pm, last entry 9.30pm; 🚊Tourist Shuttle) Melbourne's tallest building, the 297m-high Eureka Tower, was built in 2006 and a wild elevator ride takes you to its 88th floor in less than 40 seconds (check out the photo on the elevator floor if there's time). The Edge – a slightly sadistic glass cube – cantilevers you out of the building; you've got no choice but to look down.

Australian Centre for Contemporary Art   GALLERY
(ACCA; ◩03-9697 9999; www.accaonline.org.au; 111 Sturt St; ◎10am-5pm Tue & Thu-Sun, to 8pm Wed; 🚊1) FREE ACCA is one of Australia's most exciting and challenging contemporary galleries, showcasing a range of local and international artists. The building is, fittingly, sculptural, with a rusted exterior evoking the factories that once stood on the site, and a soaring interior designed to house often-massive installations. From Flinders St Station, walk across Princes Bridge and along St Kilda Rd. Turn right at Grant St, then left into Sturt St.

Polly Woodside   MUSEUM
(◩03-9699 9760; www.pollywoodside.com.au; 2a Clarendon St; adult/child/family $16/9.50/43; ◎10am-4pm Sat & Sun, daily during school holidays; 🚊96, 109, 112) The *Polly Woodside* is a restored iron-hulled merchant ship (or 'tall ship'), dating from 1885, that now rests in a pen off the Yarra River. A glimpse of the rigging makes for a tiny reminder of what the Yarra, dense with ships at anchor, would have looked like in the 19th century.

Melbourne Star   FERRIS WHEEL
(◩03-8688 9688; www.melbournestar.com; 101 Waterfront Way, Docklands; adult/child/family

Central Melbourne

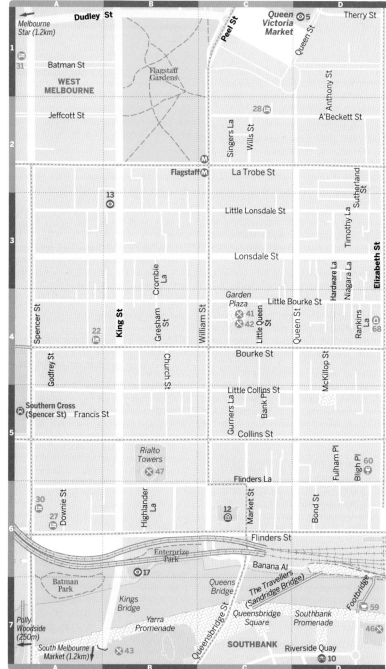

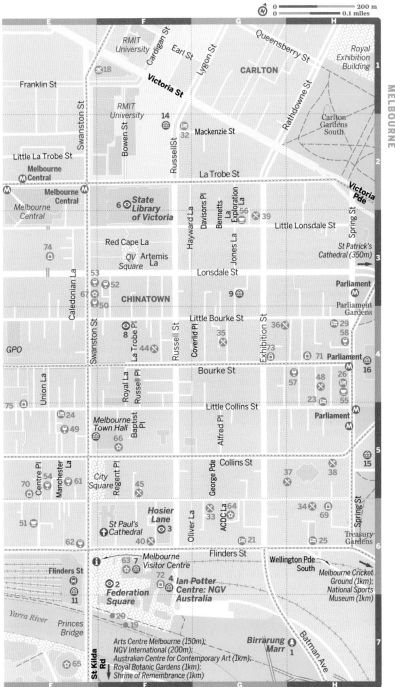

0   200 m
0   0.1 miles

Queensberry St

RMIT University
Cardigan St
Earl St
Lygon St
CARLTON

Royal Exhibition Building

Franklin St

Victoria St

Swanston St

RMIT University
Bowen St
RussellSt

14
32
Mackenzie St

Rathdowne St

Carlton Gardens South

Little La Trobe St

Melbourne Central

La Trobe St

Victoria Pde

Melbourne Central
Melbourne Central

State Library of Victoria

6

Davisons Pl
Hayward La
Bennetts La
Exploration La
56
39
Little Lonsdale St

Spring St

Red Cape La

QV Square
Artemis La

74

St Patrick's Cathedral (350m)

Caledonian La

53
52
67
50

CHINATOWN

Jones La

Lonsdale St

9

Parliament

Parliament Gardens

GPO

8
La Trobe Pl

Swanston St

Russell St

Coverlid Pl

Little Bourke St

35

Exhibition St

36

29
58

44

73

71 Parliament
16

Union La

Bourke St

57

48
26

23
55

75

Little Collins St

Alfred Pl

Parliament

24
49

Melbourne Town Hall

Baptist Pl

66

Parliament

Centre Pl
Manchester La

70
54
61

City Square

Regent Pl

45

Collins St
George Pde

37
38

15

51

St Paul's Cathedral

Hosier Lane
3

Oliver La
ACDC La

33
64

34
69

Spring St

62

40

21

25

Treasury Gardens

Flinders St

Wellington Pde South

Flinders St

63 7
Melbourne Visitor Centre

72
4 Ian Potter Centre: NGV Australia

2
Federation Square

Melbourne Cricket Ground (1km);
National Sports Museum (1km)

Yarra River
Princes Bridge

11

20
19

Arts Centre Melbourne (150m);
NGV International (200m);
Australian Centre for Contemporary Art (1km);
Royal Botanic Gardens (1km);
Shrine of Remembrance (1km)

St Kilda Rd

Birrarung Marr
1

Batman Ave

65

Central Melbourne

◎ Top Sights
1	Birrarung Marr	H7
2	Federation Square	F6
3	Hosier Lane	F6
4	Ian Potter Centre: NGV Australia	F6
5	Queen Victoria Market	D1
6	State Library of Victoria	F2

◎ Sights
7	Australian Centre for the Moving Image	F6
8	Chinatown	F4
9	Chinese Museum	G3
10	Eureka Skydeck	D7
11	Flinders Street Station	E6
12	Immigration Museum	C6
13	Koorie Heritage Trust	B3
14	Old Melbourne Gaol	F2
15	Old Treasury Building	H5
16	Parliament House	H4
17	Sea Life Melbourne Aquarium	B6

◎ Activities, Courses & Tours
18	Melbourne City Baths	F1
19	Melbourne River Cruises	F7
20	Real Melbourne Bike Tours	F7

◎ Sleeping
21	Adina Apartment Hotel	G6
22	Alto Hotel on Bourke	A4
23	City Centre Budget Hotel	H4
24	Hotel Causeway	E5
25	Hotel Lindrum	H6
26	Hotel Windsor	H4
27	Melbourne Central YHA	A6
28	Nomad's Melbourne	C2
29	Ovolo	H4
30	Pensione Hotel	A6
31	Robinsons in the City	A1
32	Space Hotel	F2

◎ Eating
33	Chin Chin	G6
34	Cumulus Inc	H6
35	Flower Drum	G4
36	Gingerboy	G4
37	Kenzan	H5
38	Mamasita	H5
39	Misschu	G3
40	MoVida	F6
41	MoVida Aqui	C4
42	Paco's Tacos	C4
43	Rockpool Bar & Grill	B7
44	ShanDong MaMa	F4
45	Supernormal	F5
46	Tutto Bene	D7
47	Vue de Monde	B5
48	Waiters Restaurant	H4

◎ Drinking & Nightlife
49	Bar Americano	E5
50	Cookie	E3
51	Degraves Espresso	E6
52	Ferdydurke	F3
53	Goldilocks	E3
54	Hell's Kitchen	E5
55	Hotel Windsor	H4
56	League of Honest Coffee	G3
	Lui Bar	(see 47)
57	Madame Brussels	H4
58	Melbourne Supper Club	H4
59	Ponyfish Island	D7
60	Robot	D5
61	Shebeen	E5
62	Young & Jackson's	E6

◎ Entertainment
63	Australian Centre for the Moving Image	F6
64	Cherry	G6
65	Hamer Hall	E7
66	Last Laugh at the Comedy Club	F5
	Melbourne Symphony Orchestra	(see 65)
67	Rooftop Cinema	E3

◎ Shopping
68	Captains of Industry	D4
69	Craft Victoria Shop	H6
70	Incu	E5
71	Melbournalia	H4
72	NGV Shop at the Ian Potter Centre	F6
73	Original & Authentic Aboriginal Art	G4
74	RM Williams	E3
75	Somewhere	E5

$32/19/82; ⊙10am-10pm; ⊡City Circle, 70, 86, ⊠Southern Cross) Originally erected in 2009, then disassembled due to structural problems before financial issues delayed it for several years more, the Melbourne Star Ferris wheel is finally turning. Joining the London Eye and Singapore Flyer, this giant observation wheel has glass cabins that take you up 120m for 360-degree views of the city, the bay and further afield to Geelong and the Dandenongs.

◎ East Melbourne & Richmond

East Melbourne's sedate, wide streets are lined with grand double-fronted Victorian terraces, Italianate mansions and art deco apartment blocks, while locals commute to the city on foot through the Fitzroy Gardens. Across perpetually clogged Punt Rd/ Hoddle St is the suburb of Richmond, which stretches all the way to the Yarra. Once a ragtag collection of workers' cottages inhabited by generations of labourers, it's now a rather genteel suburb, although it retains a fair swag of solid, regular pubs and is home to a thriving Vietnamese community along Victoria St.

★ Melbourne Cricket Ground STADIUM

(MCG; ☑ 03-9657 8888; www.mcg.org.au; Brunton Ave; tour adult/child/family $20/10/50, with National Sports Museum $30/15/70; ⊙ tours 10am-3pm; ☐ Tourist Shuttle, ☐ 48, 70, 75, ☐ Jolimont or Richmond) With a capacity of 100,000 people, the 'G' is one of the world's great sporting venues, hosting cricket in the summer and AFL footy in the winter – for many Australians it's considered hallowed ground. Make it to a game if you can (highly recommended), but otherwise you can still make a pilgrimage on non-match-day **tours** that take you through the stands, media and coaches' areas, change rooms and out onto the ground (though unfortunately not beyond the boundary).

National Sports Museum MUSEUM

(☑ 03-9657 8856; www.nsm.org.au; MCG, Olympic Stand, Gate 3; adult/concession/family $20/10/50, with MCG tour $30/15/70; ⊙ 10am-5pm) Hidden away in the bowels of the Melbourne Cricket Ground, this sports museum features five permanent exhibitions focusing on Australia's favourite sports and celebrates historic sporting moments. Kids will love the interactive sports section where they can test their footy, cricket and netball (among other sports) skills.

◉ Fitzroy & Around

Fitzroy, Melbourne's first suburb, long had a reputation for vice and squalor. Today, despite a long bout of gentrification, it's still where creative people meet up, though now it's more to 'do' lunch and blog about it before checking out the offerings at local one-off art galleries, boutiques and vintage shops.

Collingwood Children's Farm FARM

(www.farm.org.au; 18 St Heliers St, Abbotsford; adult/child/family $9/5/18; ⊙ 9.15am-4.30pm; ☐ 200, 201, 207, ☐ Victoria Park) The inner city melts away at this rustic riverside retreat beloved not just by children. There's a range of frolicking farm animals that kids can help feed, as well as rambling gardens and grounds for picnicking on warm days. The farm cafe is open early and can be visited without entering the farm itself. The monthly **farmers market** (www.mfm.com.au; 18 St Heliers St, Abbotsford; adult/child $2/free; ⊙ 8am-1pm 2nd Sat of the month), held by the river, is a local highlight.

Carlton & United Breweries BREWERY

(☑ 03-9420 6800; www.carltonbrewhouse.com.au; cnr Nelson & Thompson Sts, Abbotsford; tours adult/concession $25/20; ☐ 109) Foster's beer-brewing empire runs 1½-hour **tours** of its Abbotsford operations, where you'll encounter 30m-wide vats of beer and a super-fast bottling operation – and yes, samples are included in the price. Tours run Monday to Saturday; times vary so check the website. Visitors need to be aged over 18 and wearing closed-toed shoes. Bookings essential.

Centre for Contemporary Photography GALLERY

(CCP; Map p62; ☑ 03-9417 1549; www.ccp.org.au; 404 George St, Fitzroy; ⊙ 11am-6pm Wed-Fri, noon-5pm Sat & Sun; ☐ 86) **FREE** This not-for-profit centre has a changing schedule of photography exhibitions across a couple of galleries. Shows traverse traditional and the highly conceptual. There's a particular fascination with work involving video projection, including a nightly after-hours screening in a window. Also offers photography courses.

Alcaston Gallery GALLERY

(☑ 03-9418 6444; www.alcastongallery.com.au; 11 Brunswick St, Fitzroy; ⊙ 10am-6pm Tue-Fri, 11am-5pm Sat; ☐ 112) **FREE** Set in an imposing boom-style terrace, the Alcaston's focus is on living Indigenous Australian artists. The gallery works directly with Indigenous communities and is particularly attentive to cultural sensitivities. It shows a wide range of styles, from traditional to contemporary work. There's also a space dedicated to works on paper.

◉ Carlton & Around

Carlton is the traditional home of Melbourne's Italian community, so you'll see the *tricolori* unfurled with characteristic passion come soccer finals and the Formula One Grand Prix.

★ Melbourne Museum MUSEUM

(☑ 13 11 02; www.museumvictoria.com.au; 11 Nicholson St, Carlton; adult $12, child & student free, exhibitions extra; ⊙ 10am-5pm; ☐ Tourist Shuttle, ☐ City Circle, 86, 96, ☐ Parliament) This museum provides a grand sweep of Victoria's natural and cultural histories, with exhibitions covering everything from dinosaur fossils and giant squid specimens to a taxidermy hall, a 3D volcano and an open-air forest atrium of Victorian flora.

Royal Exhibition Building   HISTORIC BUILDING

(☑ 13 11 02; www.museumvictoria.com.au/reb; 9 Nicholson St, Carlton; tours adult/child $10/7; ☐ Tourist Shuttle, ☐ City Circle, 86, 96, ☐ Parliament) Built for the International Exhibition in 1880, and granted Unesco World Heritage status in 2004, this beautiful Victorian edifice symbolises the glory days of the Industrial Revolution, the British Empire and 19th-century Melbourne's economic supremacy. It was the first building to fly the Australian flag, and Australia's first parliament sat here in 1901. It now hosts everything from trade fairs to car shows. Tours leave from the Melbourne Museum at 2pm.

Royal Melbourne Zoo   ZOO

(☑ 03-9285 9300; www.zoo.org.au; Elliott Ave, Parkville; adult/child $30/13.20, children free on weekends & holidays; ⊙ 9am-5pm; ☐ 505, ☐ 55, ☐ Royal Park) Established in 1861, this is the oldest zoo in Australia and the third oldest in the world. Today it's one of the city's most popular attractions. Set in spacious, prettily landscaped gardens, the zoo's enclosures aim to simulate the animals' natural habitats. There's also a large collection of native animals in natural bush settings, a platypus aquarium, a fine butterfly house, fur seals, elephants, lions, tigers and plenty of reptiles.

⊙ South Yarra, Prahran & Windsor

These neighbourhoods have always been synonymous with glitz and glamour; their elevated aspect and large allotments considered prestigious. Access from the city centre to South Yarra was by boat or punt – hence Punt Rd – before Princes Bridge was built in 1850.

★ Royal Botanic Gardens   GARDENS

(www.rbg.vic.gov.au; Birdwood Ave, South Yarra; ⊙ 7.30am-sunset, Children's Garden open Wed-Sun, closed mid-Jul–mid-Sep; ☐ Tourist Shuttle, ☐ 1, 3, 5, 6, 8, 16, 64, 67, 72) FREE One of the world's finest botanic gardens, the Royal Botanical Gardens is among Melbourne's most glorious attractions. Sprawling beside the Yarra River, the beautifully designed gardens feature a global selection of plantings and specifically endemic Australian flora. Mini-ecosystems, such as a cacti and succulents area, a herb garden and an indigenous rainforest, are set amid vast lawns. Take a book, picnic or Frisbee – but most importantly, take your time.

Shrine of Remembrance   MONUMENT

(www.shrine.org.au; Birdwood Ave, South Yarra; ⊙ 10am-5pm; ☐ Tourist Shuttle, ☐ 1, 3, 5, 6, 8, 16, 64, 67, 72) FREE Beside St Kilda Rd stands the massive Shrine of Remembrance, built as a memorial to Victorians killed in WWI. It was constructed between 1928 and 1934, much of it with Depression-relief, or 'susso', labour. Its bombastic classical design is partly based on the Mausoleum of Halicarnassus, one of the seven ancient wonders of the world. Visible from the other end of town, planning regulations continue to restrict any building that would obstruct the view of the shrine from Swanston St as far back as Lonsdale St.

✦ Activities

Kayak Melbourne   KAYAKING

(☑ 0418 106 427; www.kayakmelbourne.com.au; tours $72-117; ☐ 11, 31, 48) ✦ Don't miss the chance to see the Yarra River by kayak. These two-hour tours take you past Melbourne's newest developments and explain the history of the older ones. Moonlight tours are evocative and include a dinner of fish and chips. Tours usually depart from Victoria Harbour, Docklands – check the website for directions.

Cycling

Cycling maps are available from the visitor centre in Federation Sq. The urban series includes the Main Yarra Trail (35km), off which runs the Merri Creek Trail (19km), the Outer Circle Trail (34km) and the Maribyrnong River Trail (22km). There are also paths taking you along Melbourne's beaches.

Humble Vintage   BICYCLE RENTAL

(☑ 0432 032 450; www.thehumblevintage.com; 2hr/day/week $25/35/90) ✦ Get yourself a set of special wheels from this collection of retro racers, city bikes and ladies' bikes. Rates include a lock, helmet and a terrific map with plenty of ideas about what to do with your non-bike-riding hours. Check the website for pickup locations.

Swimming

In summer, do as most Melburnians do and hit the sand at one of the city's metropolitan beaches. St Kilda, Middle Park and Port Melbourne are popular patches. Public pools are also well loved.

Melbourne City Baths   SWIMMING

(Map p58; ☑ 03-9663 5888; www.melbourne.vic.gov.au/melbournecitybaths; 420 Swanston St, Melbourne; adult/child $6.10/3.60; ⊙ 6am-10pm Mon-Thu, to 8pm Fri, 8am-6pm Sat & Sun; ☐ Melbourne Central) The City Baths were literally public baths when they first opened in 1860 and were intended to stop people bathing in and drinking from the seriously polluted Yarra

MELBOURNE ACTIVITIES

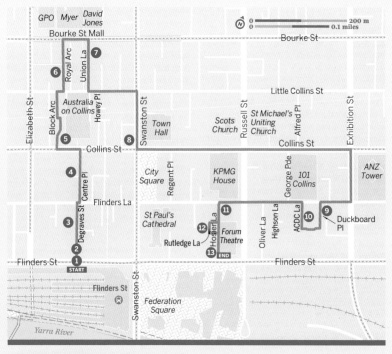

City Walk
Arcades & Lanes

START CAMPBELL ARCADE
FINISH MOVIDA
LENGTH 3KM, 2½ HOURS

Central Melbourne is a warren of 19th-century arcades and gritty-turned-hip cobbled bluestone lanes featuring street art, basement restaurants, boutiques and bars.

Start off underground at the art deco **1 Campbell Arcade**, also known as De-graves Subway, built for the '56 Olympics and now home to indie stores. Head upstairs to **2 Degraves St**, grab a coffee at **3 De-graves Espresso** and then continue north, crossing over Flinders Lane to cafe-filled **4 Centre Place**, a good place to start street-art spotting.

Cross over Collins St, turn left and enter the **5 Block Arcade**. Built in 1891 and featuring etched-glass ceilings and mosaic floors, it's based on Milan's Galleria Vittorio Emanuele plaza. Ogle the window display at the Hopetoun Tea Rooms. Exit the other end of the arcade into Little Collins St and per-

haps grab an afternoon cocktail at Chuckle Park.

Across Little Collins, head into **6 Royal Arcade** for a potter. Wander through to Bourke St Mall, then turn right and walk until you find street-art-covered **7 Union Lane** on the right.

Follow Union Lane out and turn left onto Little Collins St, then take a right on Swan-ston St and walk south to the **8 Manchester Unity Arcade** (1932) on the corner of Collins St. Take a look in this beautiful arcade, then go back out to Swanston and head east, up the hill, to the 'Paris End' of Collins St.

Turn right into Exhibition St, then right into Flinders Lane and continue until you see **9 Duckboard Place**. Head down the lane, taking time to soak up the street art before horseshoeing around into ACDC Lane, past rock 'n' roll dive bar **10 Cherry** (p75).

Continue down Flinders Lane to the street-art meccas of **11 Hosier Lane** (p53) and **12 Rutledge Lane** before finishing with tapas and a hard-earned drink at **13 MoVida** (p68).

River. They now boast the city centre's largest pool (30m), plus you can do your laps in a 1903 heritage-listed building.

Melbourne Sports & Aquatic Centre
SWIMMING

(MSAC; ☑03-9926 1555; www.msac.com.au; Albert Rd, Albert Park; adult/child $7.40/5.20; ☺5.30am-10pm Mon-Fri, 7am-8pm Sat & Sun; ⊟96, 112) Has a fantastic indoor 50m pool, wave pool, water slides, spa-sauna-steam room and spacious common areas, on the shore of Albert Park Lake.

Windsurfing, Kiteboarding & Stand-Up Paddle Boarding

Kiteboarding has a fast-emerging scene around St Kilda between November and April. Elwood, just south of St Kilda, is a popular sailboarding area.

Stand Up Paddle HQ
WATER SPORTS

(☑0416 184 994; www.supb.com.au; St Kilda Pier; hire per hr $30, 2hr tour $89; ⊟96) Arrange a lesson, hire SUP equipment, or join a Yarra River tour.

Kite Republic
KITESURFING

(☑03-9537 0644; www.kiterepublic.com.au; St Kilda Seabaths, 4/10-18 Jacka Blvd; 1hr lesson $90; ☺10am-7pm) Offers kiteboarding lessons, tours and equipment; also a good source of info. In winter it can arrange snow-kiting at Mt Hotham. Also rents SUPs and Street SUPs.

👉 Tours

Melbourne By Foot
WALKING TOUR

(☑0418 394 000; www.melbournebyfoot.com; tours $40; ⊞Flinders St) 🍃 Take a few hours out and experience a mellow, informative 4km walking tour that covers lane art, politics, Melbourne's history and diversity. Tours include a refreshment break. There's also the enticing Beer Lovers' Guide to Melbourne. Highly recommended; book online.

Aboriginal Heritage Walk
CULTURAL TOUR

(☑03-9252 2300; www.rbg.vic.gov.au; adult/child $25/10; ☺11am Sun-Thu; ⊟Tourist Shuttle, ⊟8) 🍃 The Royal Botanic Gardens are on a traditional camping and meeting place of the original Indigenous owners, and this tour takes you through their story – from songlines to plant lore, in all 90 fascinating minutes. The tour departs from the visitor centre.

Melbourne Street Art Tours
WALKING TOUR

(☑03-9328 5556; www.melbournestreettours.com; tours $69; ☺1.30pm Tue, Thu & Sat) 🍃 Three-hour tours exploring the street-art side of

Melbourne. The tour guides are street artists themselves, so you'll get a good insight into this art form.

Real Melbourne Bike Tours
BICYCLE TOUR

(Map p58; ☑0417 339 203; www.rentabike.net.au/biketours; Federation Sq; 4hr tour incl lunch adult/child $110/79; ☺10am; ⊞Flinders St) 🍃 These bike tours allow you to cover more ground on a well-thought-out itinerary that provides a local's insight to Melbourne, with a foodie focus. Rents bikes, too.

Hidden Secrets Tours
WALKING TOUR

(☑03-9663 3358; www.hiddensecretstours.com; tours $29-150) 🍃 Offers a variety of walking tours covering subjects such as lanes and arcades, wine, architecture, coffee and cafes, and vintage Melbourne.

Melbourne Visitor Shuttle
BUS TOUR

(Tourist Shuttle; www.thatsmelbourne.com.au; daily ticket $5, children under 10 free; ☺9.30am-4.30pm) This bus runs a 1½-hour round-trip route, with audio commentary and 13 stops that take in all of Melbourne's main sights.

Melbourne River Cruises
BOAT TOUR

(Map p58; ☑03-9681 3284; www.melbcruises.com.au; Federation Wharf; adult/child from $23/11) Take a one-hour cruise upstream or downstream along the Yarra River, or a 2½-hour return cruise, departing from a couple of locations – check for details. It also operates a ferry between Southgate and Gem Pier in Williamstown, sailing three to nine times daily, depending on the season.

🎊 Festivals & Events

Australian Open
SPORTS

(www.australianopen.com; National Tennis Centre; ☺Jan) The world's top tennis players and huge merry-making crowds descend for Australia's Grand Slam tennis championship.

Midsumma Festival
GAY & LESBIAN

(www.midsumma.org.au) Melbourne's annual gay-and-lesbian arts festival features more than 100 events from mid-January to mid-February, with a Pride March finale.

Chinese New Year
CULTURAL

(www.chinatownmelbourne.com.au; Little Bourke St; ☺Feb) Melbourne has celebrated the lunar new year since Little Bourke St became Chinatown in the 1860s.

White Night
CULTURAL

(www.whitenightmelbourne.com.au; ☺Feb) Melbourne's annual all-night event where the city is illuminated in colourful projections, forming a backdrop to free art, music and film.

Melbourne Food & Wine Festival
FOOD

(www.melbournefoodandwine.com.au; ☺ Mar) Market tours, wine tastings, cooking classes and presentations by celeb chefs take place at venues across the city (and state).

Moomba
CULTURAL

(www.thatsmelbourne.com.au; Alexandra Gardens; ☺ Mar) A waterside festival famous locally for its wacky Birdman Rally, where competitors launch themselves into the Yarra in homemade flying machines.

Australian Formula One Grand Prix
SPORTS

(☎ 1800 100 030; www.grandprix.com.au; Albert Park; tickets from $55; ☺ Mar) The 5.3km street circuit around the normally tranquil Albert Park Lake is known for its smooth, fast surface. The buzz, both on the streets and in your ears, takes over Melbourne for four days of rev-head action.

Melbourne International Comedy Festival
COMEDY

(www.comedyfestival.com.au; Melbourne Town Hall; ☺ Mar-Apr) An enormous range of local and international comic talent hits town with four weeks of laughs.

Melbourne Jazz
JAZZ

(www.melbournejazz.com; ☺ May-Jun) International jazz cats head to town and join locals for gigs at Hamer Hall, the Regent Theatre and the Palms at Crown Casino.

Melbourne International Film Festival
FILM

(MIFF; miff.com.au; ☺ Jul-Aug) Midwinter movie love-in brings out black-skivvy-wearing cinephiles in droves.

Melbourne Writers Festival
LITERATURE

(www.mwf.com.au; ☺ Aug) Yes, Melbourne is a Unesco City of Literature and it's proud of its writers and, indeed, readers. Beginning in the last week of August, the Writers Festival features forums and events at various venues.

AFL Grand Final
SPORTS

(www.afl.com.au; MCG; ☺ Sep) It's easier to kick a goal from the boundary line than to pick up tickets to the grand final, but it's not hard to get your share of finals fever anywhere in Melbourne (particularly at pubs).

Melbourne International Arts Festival
ART

(www.melbournefestival.com.au; ☺ Oct) Held at various venues around the city, this festival features a thought-provoking program of Australian and international theatre, opera, dance, visual art and music.

Chinese New Year celebrations

Melbourne Cup `SPORTS`

(www.springracingcarnival.com.au; ☉Nov) Culminating in the prestigious Melbourne Cup, the Spring Racing Carnival is as much a social event as a sporting one. The Cup, held on the first Tuesday in November, is a public holiday in Melbourne.

Boxing Day Test `SPORTS`

(www.mcg.org.au; MCG; ☉Dec) Boxing Day is day one of Melbourne's annually scheduled international Test cricket match, drawing out the cricket fans. Expect some shenanigans from Bay 13.

🛏 Sleeping

🛏 Central Melbourne

There are a lot of places across all price ranges that will put you in the heart of the action.

★ Space Hotel `HOSTEL, HOTEL $`

(Map p58; ☑03-9662 3888; www.spacehotel.com. au; 380 Russell St; dm/s/d without bathroom from $29/77/93; ☀@☎; ☐City Circle, 24, 30) One of Melbourne's few genuine flashpackers, this sleek, modern and immaculate hotel has something for all demographics, all at very reasonable prices. Rooms have iPod docks and flat-screen TVs, while dorms have thoughtful touches such as large lockers equipped with sensor lights and lockable adapters. A few doubles have en suites and balconies.

Melbourne Central YHA `HOSTEL $`

(Map p58; ☑03-9621 2523; www.yha.com.au; 562 Flinders St; dm/d $34/100; @☎; ☐70) This heritage building has been totally transformed by the YHA gang with a recent overhaul making it even better. Expect a lively reception, handsome rooms, and kitchens and common areas on each of the four levels. Entertainment's high on the agenda, and there's a fab restaurant called Bertha Brown on the ground floor and a grand rooftop area.

Nomad's Melbourne `HOSTEL $`

(Map p58; ☑03-9328 4383; www.nomadshostels. com; 198 A'Beckett St; dm $20-45, d $100-145; P@☎; ☐Flagstaff) Flashpacking hits Melbourne's city centre with this smart hostel boasting a mix of four- to 14-bed dorms (some with en suite) and spacious doubles. There's a rooftop area with BBQ, cinema lounge, bar and plenty of gloss (especially in the females-only wing).

City Centre Budget Hotel `HOTEL $`

(Map p58; ☑03-9654 5401; www.citycentre budgethotel.com.au; 22 Little Collins St; d with shared/private bathroom from $79/94; @☎; ☐Parliament) Intimate, independent and inconspicuous, this 38-room budget hotel is a find. It's located up some stairs inside an unassuming building. Rooms are no-frills yet neat and tidy, staff are ultra-friendly and there's free wi-fi, a laundry and communal kitchen on the pebbled rooftop.

★ Adina Apartment Hotel `APARTMENT $$`

(Map p58; ☑03-8663 0000; www.adinahotels.com. au; 88 Flinders St; apt from $141; P☀☎; ☐City Circle, 70, 75) Quintessential Melbourne, these designer, cool monochromatic warehouse-style loft apartments are extra large and luxurious. Ask for one at the front for amazing parkland views or get glimpses into Melbourne's lanes from the giant polished-floorboard studios, all with full kitchens. Also has apartments in St Kilda (☑03-9536 0000; 157 Fitzroy St, St Kilda; apt from $139) overlooking Albert Park.

Alto Hotel on Bourke `HOTEL $$`

(Map p58; ☑03-8608 5500; www.altohotel. com.au; 636 Bourke St; r from $166; P☀@☎; ☐86, 96) 🖉 Environment-minded Alto has water-saving showers, energy-efficient lights and double-glazed windows, and in-room recycling is encouraged. Rooms are also well equipped, with good light and neutral decor. Apartments (but not studios) have full kitchens and multiple LCD TVs, and some have spas. Freebies include organic espresso coffee, apples and access to a massage room. Guests can use an electric car for $17 per hour.

Pensione Hotel `HOTEL $$`

(Map p58; ☑03-9621 3333; www.pensione.com. au; 16 Spencer St; r from $114; P☀@☎; ☐96, 109, 112) With refreshing honesty, the lovely, boutique Pensione Hotel names some rooms as 'shoebox' and 'matchbox' – but what you don't get in size is more than made up for in spot-on style, room extras and super-reasonable rates.

Hotel Causeway `HOTEL $$`

(Map p58; ☑03-9660 8888; www.causeway.com. au; 275 Little Collins St; r from $139; ☀@☎; ☐86, 96) With a discreet entrance in the Howey Place covered arcade, Causeway will appeal to those who've come to Melbourne to shop and bar hop. It's intimate in scale, so don't expect the facilities of a big hotel. Rooms are boutiquey and feature luxurious linen, robes and slippers.

Robinsons in the City BOUTIQUE HOTEL $$
(Map p58; ☑03-9329 2552; www.ritc.com.au; 405 Spencer St; r from $149; P ❋ 🕾; 🚊75, 96) Robinsons is a gem, with six large rooms and warm service. The building is a former bakery, dating from 1850, but it's been given a modern, eclectic look. Bathrooms are not in the rooms; each room has its own in the hall. Service is warm and personal, and repeat visits are common.

★ Ovolo BOUTIQUE HOTEL $$$
(Map p58; ☑03-8692 0777; www.ovologroup.com; 19 Little Bourke St; r incl breakfast from $215; P ❋ @ 🕾; 🚇Parliament) Melbourne's newest boutique hotel mixes hipster chic with a funky executive vibe. It's friendly, fun and loaded with goodies – there's a free minibar in each room, and free booze downstairs at the daily happy hour. Throw in a 'goodie bag' on arrival, Nespresso machine in the lobby and Le Patisserie breakfast pastries and you'll be wanting to move in permanently.

Hotel Lindrum BOUTIQUE HOTEL $$$
(Map p58; ☑03-9668 1111; www.hotellindrum.com. au; 26 Flinders St; r from $275; P ❋ 🕾; 🚊70, 75) One of the city's most attractive hotels, this was once the snooker hall of the legendary and literally unbeatable Walter Lindrum. Expect rich tones, subtle lighting and tactile fabrics. Spring for a deluxe room and you'll snare either arch or bay windows and marvellous Melbourne views. And yes, there's a billiard table – one of Lindrum's originals, no less.

Crown Metropol HOTEL $$$
(☑03-9292 6211; www.crownhotels.com.au; Crown Casino, 8 Whiteman St; r from $280; ❋ @ 🕾 ⛫; 🚊96, 109, 112) The most boutique of Crown's hotels, guests here have access to the most extraordinary infinity pool in Melbourne, with 270-degree views over the city to the Dandenongs in the distance. The beautifully appointed luxe twin rooms are the least expensive on offer and sleep four.

Hotel Windsor HOTEL $$$
(Map p58; ☑03-9633 6000; www.thehotelwind sor.com.au; 111 Spring St; r from $200; ❋ @; 🚇Parliament) Sparkling chandeliers and a grand piano in the lobby set the scene for this opulent, heritage-listed 1883 building that's one of Australia's most famous and self-consciously grand hotels. It was still awaiting

a controversial $260 million redevelopment at time of research. Adding to its English quaintness is high tea service (p72) and the historic Cricketers Bar, decked out in cricketing memorabilia.

🛏 East Melbourne & Fitzroy

These areas takes you out of the action, yet are still walking distance from the city and offer ready access to the MCG.

★ Nunnery HOSTEL $
(☑03-9419 8637; www.nunnery.com.au; 116 Nicholson St, Fitzroy; dm/s/d incl breakfast from $32/90/120; @ 🕾; 🚊96) Built in 1888, the Nunnery oozes atmosphere, with sweeping staircases and many original features – the walls are dripping with religious works of art and ornate stained-glass windows. You'll be giving thanks for the big comfortable lounges and communal areas. Next door to the main building is the Nunnery Guesthouse, which has larger rooms in a private setting (from $130). It's perennially popular, so book ahead.

Brooklyn Arts Hotel BOUTIQUE HOTEL $$
(☑03-9419 9328; www.brooklynartshotel.com. au; 48-50 George St, Fitzroy; s/d incl breakfast from $115/155; 🕾; 🚊86) There are seven very different rooms in this character-filled and very unique hotel. Owner Maggie has put the call out for artistic people and they've responded by staying, so expect lively conversation around the continental breakfast. Rooms vary in size, but all are clean, quirky, colourful and beautifully decorated; one even houses a piano. Spacious upstairs rooms with high ceilings and street views are the pick.

🛏 South Yarra & Prahran

South of the river, South Yarra has some tremendous boutique and upmarket places set in pretty, tree-lined residential streets.

★ Art Series (The Cullen) BOUTIQUE HOTEL $$$
(☑03-9098 1555; www.artserieshotels.com.au/ cullen; 164 Commercial Rd, Prahran; r from $215; ❋ @ 🕾; 🚊72, 78, 79, 🚇Prahran) The edgiest of the Art Series hotels, this one's decked out by the late grunge painter Adam Cullen, whose vibrant and often graphic works provide visions of Ned Kelly shooting you from the glam opaque room/bathroom dividers. Rooms are classic boutique – ultra-comfy but not big on space.

✕ Eating

✕ Central Melbourne

★ ShanDong MaMa
ASIAN $

(Map p58; ☏03-9650 3818; shop 7, Mid City Arcade, 200 Bourke St; mains from $11; ⏰11am-9pm) Melbourne's passion for dumplings finds its truest expression in this simple little place. Dumplings here are boiled, rather than steamed as they are elsewhere, and arrive any later than noon for lunch and you'll have to wait. Our favourite order for two is a plate of Little Rachaels and another of King Prawn dumplings. Bliss.

Miss Katie's Crab Shack
AMERICAN $

(☏03-9329 9888; www.misskatiescrabshack.com; 238 Victoria St; dishes $8-25; ⏰5-9pm Tue-Fri, noon-9pm Sat, noon-8pm Sun; ☐19, 57, 59) Set up inside the Public Bar, Miss Katie's shack puts a twist on pub food through her Southern home-style cooking, using fresh produce from the Vic Market across the road and homemade hot sauces. Thank her grandma from Virginia for the signature fried chicken, and her mum from Maryland for the Chesapeake Bay–style blue swimmer crab dishes.

Misschu
SOUTHEAST ASIAN $

(Map p58; ☏03-9077 1097; www.misschu.com.au; 297 Exhibition St; mains $7-16; ⏰11am-10pm; ☐City Circle, 24, 30) The self-proclaimed 'queen of rice paper rolls', Misschu continues to expand her empire of hole-in-the-wall eateries serving cheap and tasty Laotian-Vietnamese hawker-style food and furnished in eclectic design, with wooden-crate seating and 1950s retro blinds. Fill out your order form for roast-duck-and-banana-flower rice paper rolls, or beef and oxtail pho. It's in South Yarra (Map p66; ☏03-9041 5848; 276 Toorak Rd, South Yarra; ⏰11am-11pm; ☐8, 78, 79), too.

★ MoVida
SPANISH $$

(Map p58; ☏03-9663 3038; www.movida.com.au; 1 Hosier Lane; tapas $4-6, raciones $8-30; ⏰noon-late; ☐70, 75, ☐Flinders St) MoVida sits in a cobbled lane emblazoned with one of the world's densest collections of street art – it doesn't get much more Melbourne than this. Line up along the bar, cluster around little window tables or, if you've booked, take a table in the dining area for fantastic Spanish tapas and *raciones*.

MoVida Next Door – yes, right next door – is the perfect place for a pre-show beer and tapas. Also brought to you by MoVida is MoVida Aqui (Map p58; ☏03-9663 3038; www.movida.com.au; 1st fl, 500 Bourke St; tapas from $4.50, raciones $22-30; ⏰noon-late Mon-Fri, 6pm-late Sat; ☐86, 96), a huge, open space with a similar tapas menu and chargrilled cooking, while next door is its Mexican offering of Paco's Tacos (Map p58; ☏03-9663 3038; www.pacostacos.com.au; 1st fl, 500 Bourke St; tacos $6; ⏰noon-11pm; ☐86, 96). It's also recently opened Bar Pulpo (www. movida.com.au/airport; Terminal 2, Melbourne Airport; breakfast $7.90-22.50, tapas from $4.90,

A race that stops the nation – the Melbourne Cup (p66)

raciones from $13.90; ⊙8am-12.30am) at Melbourne Airport for pre-flight tapas and drinks.

★ Supernormal ASIAN $$

(Map p58; ☑03-9650 8688; www.supernormal. net.au; 180 Flinders Lane; mains $15-37; ⊙11am-11pm Sun-Thu, to midnight Fri & Sat) Andrew McConnell can, it seems, do no wrong. Drawing on his years spent living and cooking in Shanghai and Hong Kong, McConnell presents a creative selection, from dumplings to raw seafood and mains such as slow-cooked Szechuan lamb. Even if you don't dine in, stop by for his now-famous takeaway New England lobster roll – lobster in a small brioche...what's not to like? No dinner bookings for five or less people.

Mamasita MEXICAN $$

(Map p58; ☑03-9650 3821; www.mamasita.com. au; 1/11 Collins St; tacos from $5, shared plates from $19; ⊙noon-late Mon-Sat, from 1pm Sun; ☐City Circle, 11, 31, 48, 112) The restaurant responsible for kicking off Melbourne's obsession with authentic Mexican street food, Mamasita is still one of the very best – as evidenced by the perpetual queues to get into the place. The chargrilled corn sprinkled with cheese and chipotle mayo is a legendary starter, and there's a fantastic range of corn-tortilla tacos and 180 types of tequila. No reservations, so prepare to wait.

Cumulus Inc MODERN AUSTRALIAN $$

(Map p58; www.cumulusinc.com.au; 45 Flinders Lane; mains $19-39; ⊙7am-11pm Mon-Fri, from 8am Sat & Sun; ☐City Circle, 48) One of Melbourne's best for any meal, giving you that wonderful Andrew McConnell–style along with reasonable prices. The focus is on beautiful produce and simple but artful cooking, from breakfasts of sardines and smoked tomato on toast at the marble bar, to suppers of freshly shucked clair de lune oysters tucked away on the leather banquettes. No reservations, so queues are highly probable.

Chin Chin ASIAN $$

(Map p58; ☑03-8663 2000; www.chinchinres taurant.com.au; 125 Flinders Lane; mains $19-33; ⊙11am-late; ☐City Circle, 70, 75) Yet another great option on Flinders Lane, Chin Chin does delicious Southeast Asian hawker-style food designed as shared plates. It's inside a busied-up shell of an old building with a real New York feel, and while there are no book-

ings, Go Go Bar downstairs will have you till there's space.

★ Vue de Monde MODERN AUSTRALIAN $$$

(Map p58; ☑03-9691 3888; www.vuedemonde. com.au; level 55, Rialto, 525 Collins St; set menus $150-250; ⊙reservations from noon-2pm Tue-Fri & Sun, 6-9.15pm Mon-Sat; ☐11, 31, 48, 109, 112, ☐Southern Cross) Sitting pretty in the old observation deck of the Rialto, Melbourne's favoured spot for occasion dining has views to match its name. Visionary chef Shannon Bennett has moved away from its classic French style to a subtle Modern Australian theme that runs through everything from the decor to the menu.

★ Kenzan JAPANESE $$$

(Map p58; ☑03-9654 8933; www.kenzan.com.au; 56 Flinders St; mains $30-45, lunch/dinner set menu from $36/85; ⊙noon-2.30pm & 6-10pm) One of numerous candidates for the title of Melbourne's best Japanese restaurant, Kenzan inhabits an unpromising setting but serves up sublime sashimi and sushi, with the nabe ryori (which you cook at your table) another fine option. Can't choose? Lunch and dinner set menus are outstanding. Order the more expensive marbled beef when given the choice.

Flower Drum CHINESE $$$

(Map p58; ☑03-9662 3655; www.flower-drum. com; 17 Market Lane; mains $15-60; ⊙noon-3pm & 6-11pm Mon-Sat, 6-10.30pm Sun; ☎; ☐86, 96) The Flower Drum continues to be Melbourne's most celebrated Chinese restaurant. The finest, freshest produce prepared with absolute attention to detail keeps this Chinatown institution booked out weeks in advance. The sumptuous, but ostensibly simple, Cantonese food (from a menu that changes daily) is delivered with the slick service you'd expect in such elegant surrounds.

Gingerboy ASIAN $$$

(Map p58; ☑03-9662 4200; www.gingerboy. com.au; 27-29 Crossley St; shared dishes $32-52; ⊙noon-2.30pm & 5.30-10.30pm Mon-Fri, 5.30-10.30pm Sat; ☐86, 96) Brave the aggressively trendy surrounds and weekend party scene, as talented Teague Ezard does a fine turn in flash hawker cooking. Flavours pop in dishes such as scallops with green chilli jam or coconut kingfish with peanut and tamarind dressing. There are two dinner sittings; bookings are required. Upstairs, Gingerboy has a long, long cocktail bar.

✘ Southgate, South Wharf & the Docklands

Tutto Bene   ITALIAN $$
(Map p58; ☑ 03-9696 3334; www.tuttobene.net.au; midlevel, Southgate; mains $24-45; ⊗ noon-3pm & 6-10pm; ⓡ Flinders St) This Italian restaurant is especially known for its risotto dishes, which range from a simple Venetian *risi e bisi* (rice and peas) to some fabulously luxe options involving truffles, roast quail or aged balsamic. Don't miss its fine house-made gelato.

Rockpool Bar & Grill   STEAK $$$
(Map p58;   ☑ 03-8648 1900;   www.rockpool melbourne.com; Crown Entertainment Complex; mains $24-110; ⊗ noon-2.30pm Sun-Fri, 6-11pm daily; ⓡ 55, ⓡ Flinders St) The Melbourne outpost of Neil Perry's empire offers his signature seafood raw bar, but it's really all about beef, from grass-fed to full-blood Wagyu. The darkly masculine space is simple and stylish, as is the menu. The bar offers the same level of food service, with the added bonus of a rather spectacular drinks menu.

✘ Richmond

Richmond Hill Cafe & Larder   CAFE $$
(☑ 03-9421 2808; www.rhcl.com.au; 48-50 Bridge Rd; lunch $12-30; ⊗ 8am-5pm; ⓡ 75, ⓡ West Richmond) Once the domain of well-known cook Stephanie Alexander, it still boasts its lovely cheese room and simple, comforting foods such as cheesy toast. There are breakfast cocktails for the brave.

✘ Fitzroy & Around

Po' Boy Quarter   AMERICAN $
(☑ 03-9419 2130;   www.gumbokitchen.com.au; 295 Smith St, Fitzroy; rolls $10-14; ⊗ 11.30am-1am; ⓡ 86) The boys behind the Gumbo Kitchen truck have parked permanently on Smith St with this smart canteen-style eatery. Wolf down one of their rolls of pulled pork, shrimp with Louisiana hot sauce, or fried green tomatoes with Cajun slaw while people watching out front.

Jimmy Grants   GREEK $
(www.jimmygrants.com.au; 113 St David St, Fitzroy; souvlakis from $9; ⊗ 11am-10pm; ⓡ 86) Set up by celebrity chef George Calombaris, this is not your ordinary souva joint – these are gourmet souvlakis, which you don't need to be plastered at 3am to enjoy. Options may include a pita stuffed with lamb, mustard aioli and chips, or honey prawn and herbs.

★Charcoal Lane   MODERN AUSTRALIAN $$
(☑ 03-9418 3400; www.charcoallane.com.au; 136 Gertrude St, Fitzroy; mains $19-31; ⊗ noon-3pm & 6-9pm Tue-Sat; ⓡ 86) 🍷 Housed in an old bluestone former bank, this training restaurant for Indigenous and disadvantaged young people is one of the best places to try native flora and fauna – menu items may include kangaroo burger with bush tomato chutney and wallaby tartare. Weekend bookings advised. It also holds cooking masterclasses using native ingredients; check the website for details.

Añada   TAPAS $$
(☑ 03-9415 6101; www.anada.com.au; 197 Gertrude St, Fitzroy; tapas from $4, raciones $10-26; ⊗ 5pm-late Mon-Fri, noon-late Sat & Sun; ⓡ 86) Dishes in this lovely little restaurant are alive with hearty Spanish and Muslim-Mediterranean flavours. It has a great tapas selection, or go the nine-course banquet (chef's choice) for $50.

Cutler & Co   MODERN AUSTRALIAN $$$
(☑ 03-9419 4888; www.cutlerandco.com.au; 55 Gertrude St, Fitzroy; mains $36-49; ⊗ noon-late Fri & Sun, 6pm-late Mon-Thu; ⓡ 86) Hyped for all the right reasons, this is another of Andrew McConnell's restaurants and though its decor might be a little over the top, its attentive, informed staff and joy-inducing dishes (roast suckling pig, Earl Grey ice cream and Moonlight Bay oysters, to name a few) have quickly made this one of Melbourne's best.

✘ Carlton & Around

Sugardough Panificio & Patisserie   BAKERY $
(☑ 03-9380 4060; www.sugardough.com.au; 163 Lygon St, East Brunswick; mains $8.60; ⊗ 7.30am-5pm Tue-Fri, to 4pm Sat & Sun; ⓡ 1, 8) Sugardough does a roaring trade in homemade pies (including vegetarian ones), home-baked bread and pastries. Mismatched cutlery and cups and saucers make it rather like being at Grandma's on family reunion day.

D.O.C Espresso   ITALIAN $$
(☑ 03-9347 8482; www.docgroup.net; 326 Lygon St, Carlton; mains $12-20; ⊗ 7.30am-9.30pm Mon-Sat, 8am-9pm Sun; ⓡ 205, ⓡ 1, 8, 96) Run by third-generation Italians, D.O.C is bringing authenticity, and breathing new life, back into Lygon St. The espresso bar features homemade pasta specials, Italian microbrewery beers and *aperitivo* time (4pm to 7pm),

where you can enjoy a Negroni cocktail with complimentary nibble board while surrounded by dangling legs of meat and huge wheels of cheese behind glass shelves.

The **deli** (☑03-9347 8482; www.docgroup.net; 326 Lygon St, Carlton; mains from $12; ⊙9am-8pm) next door does great cheese boards and panini, while around the corner is D.O.C's original **pizzeria** (☑03-9347 2998; www.docgroup.net; 295 Drummond St, Carlton; pizzas around $13-18; ⊙5.30-10.30pm Mon-Wed, noon-10.30pm Fri-Sun; ⊡205, ⊡1, 8), with excellent thin-crust pizzas and a convivial atmosphere.

Rumi   MIDDLE EASTERN $$

(☑03-9388 8255; www.rumirestaurant.com.au; 116 Lygon St, East Brunswick; mains $12-24; ⊙6-10pm; ⊡1,8) A fabulously well-considered place that serves up a mix of traditional Lebanese cooking and contemporary interpretations of old Persian dishes. The *sigara boregi* (cheese and pine-nut pastries) are a local institution, and tasty mains such as meatballs are balanced with a large and interesting selection of vegetable dishes (the near-caramelised cauliflower and the broad beans are standouts).

Auction Rooms   CAFE $$

(☑03-9326 7749; www.auctionroomscafe.com.au; 103-107 Errol St, North Melbourne; mains $14-22; ⊙7am-5pm Mon-Fri, from 7.30am Sat & Sun; ☎; ⊡57) This former auction house–turned–North Melbourne success story serves up some of Melbourne's best coffee, both espresso and filter, using ever-changing, house-roasted, single-origin beans. Then there's its food, with a highly seasonal menu of creative breakfasts and lunches. From Queen Vic Market, head west along Victoria St, then right at Errol St.

✖ South Melbourne, Port Melbourne & Albert Park

Andrew's Burgers   BURGERS $

(☑03-9690 2126; www.andrewshamburgers.com.au; 144 Bridport St, Albert Park; burgers from $7.50; ⊙11am-3pm & 4.30-9pm Mon-Sat; ⊡1) Andrew's is a family-run burger institution that's been around since the '50s. Walls are still wood-panelled and now covered with photos of local celebs who, like many, drop in for a classic burger with the lot and a big bag of chips to takeaway. Veg option available.

St Ali   CAFE $$

(☑03-9689 2990; www.stali.com.au; 12-18 Yarra Pl, South Melbourne; dishes $8-23; ⊙7am-6pm; ⊡112) A hideaway warehouse conversion where the

coffee is carefully sourced and guaranteed to be good. If you can't decide between house blend, speciality, black or white, there's a tasting plate ($18). Awarded best food cafe in *The Age Good Cafe Guide 2013* – the corn fritters with poached eggs/haloumi are famous.

⬤ Drinking & Nightlife

Melbourne's bars are legendary, from lane hideaways to brassy corner establishments. The same goes for coffee. Out of the city centre, shopping strips are embedded with shopfront drinking holes: try Fitzroy, Collingwood, Northcote, Prahran and St Kilda. Many inner-city pubs have pushed out the barflies, pulled up the beer-stained carpet, polished the concrete and brought in talented chefs and mixologists, but don't dismiss the character-filled oldies that still exist.

⬤ Central Melbourne

★ **Bar Americano**   COCKTAIL BAR

(Map p58; 20 Pesgrave Pl, off Howey Pl; ⊙8.30am-1am; ⊡11, 31, 48, 109, 112) A hideaway bar in a city alleyway, Bar Americano is a standing-room-only affair with black-and-white chequered floors complemented with classic 'do not spit' subway tiled walls and the subtle air of a speakeasy. By day it serves excellent coffee, but after dark it's all about the cocktails; they don't come cheap but they do come superb.

Lui Bar   COCKTAIL BAR

(Map p58; www.vuedemonde.com.au; level 55, Rialto, 525 Collins St; ⊙5.30pm-midnight Mon, noon-midnight Tue-Fri, 5.30pm-late Sat, noon-evening Sun; ⊡11, 31, 48, 109, 112, ⊠Southern Cross) One of the city's most sophisticated bars, Lui offers the chance to sample the views and excellent snacks without having to indulge in the whole Vue de Monde dining experience. Suits and jet-setters cram in most nights so get there early (nicely dressed), claim your table and order drinks from the pop-up-book menu. Drinks include macadamia martinis – vacuum distilled at the bar.

Melbourne Supper Club   BAR

(Map p58; ☑03-9654 6300; 1st fl, 161 Spring St; ⊙5pm-4am Sun-Thu, to 6am Fri & Sat; ⊡95, 96, ⊠Parliament) Melbourne's own Betty Ford's (the place you go there's nowhere left to go), the Supper Club is open very late and is a favoured after-work spot for performers and hospitality types. It's entered through an unsigned wooden door, where you can leave your coat before cosying into a chesterfield. Browse the encyclopedic wine menu and relax; the sommeliers will cater to any liquid desire.

Madame Brussels
BAR

(Map p58; www.madamebrussels.com; level 3, 59-63 Bourke St; ⊗noon-1am; 🚋86, 96) Head here if you've had it with Melbourne-moody and all that dark wood. Although named for a famous 19th-century brothel owner, it feels like a camp '60s rabbit hole, with much AstroTurfery and staff dressed à la country club. It's just the tonic to escape the city for a jug of Madame Brussels–style Pimms on its wonderful rooftop terrace.

Hell's Kitchen
BAR

(Map p58; level 1, 20 Centre Pl; ⊗noon-10pm Mon & Tues, to late Wed-Sat, to 11pm Sun; 🚉Flinders St) A hidden lane bar located in the beautiful Centre Place Arcade, Hell's is up a narrow flight of stairs where you can sip on classic cocktails (Negroni, whisky sour and martinis), beer or cider and people watch from the large windows. Attracts a young, hip crowd and also serves food.

Shebeen
BAR

(Map p58; www.shebeen.com.au; 36 Manchester Lane; ⊗noon-late Mon-Fri, 4pm-late Sat; 🚋11, 31, 48, 109, 112) 🍴 Corrugated-iron walls and awnings give this relaxed bar a canteen-shack feel. Shebeen (the name for illegal drinking bars in South Africa during apartheid) offers a place to have a tipple without feeling too guilty about it – 100% of all drink profits go towards a charity partner overseas. At the time of research there were plans for live music and DJs.

Hotel Windsor
TEAHOUSE

(Map p58; www.thehotelwindsor.com.au; 111 Spring St; afternoon tea Mon-Fri $69, Sat & Sun $89; ⊗noon Mon & Tue, noon & 2.30pm Wed-Sun; 🚉Parliament) This grand hotel has been serving afternoon tea since 1883. Indulge in the delights of its three-tier platters of finger sandwiches, scones, pastries and champagne, hosted in either its front dining room or the art nouveau ballroom.

Cookie
BAR

(Map p58; ☑03-9663 7660; www.cookie.net.au; level 1, Curtin House, 252 Swanston St; ⊗noon-1am Sun-Thu, to 3am Fri & Sat) Part swanky bar, part Thai restaurant, Cookie does both exceptionally well and is one of the more enduring rites of passage of the Melbourne night.

The bar is unbelievably well stocked with fine whiskies and wines, with plenty of craft beers among the 200-plus brews on offer. It also knows how to make a serious cocktail.

Goldilocks
BAR

(Map p58; ☑0401 174 962; www.goldliocksbar.com; level 4, 262 Swanston St; ⊗2pm-3am) Fabulous cocktails (whisky with chilli anyone?) and a brilliant rooftop setting make this one of the stars of the Melbourne night and there's no reason to think the crowds will go elsewhere.

Ferdydurke
BAR

(Map p58; ☑03-9639 3750; www.ferdydurke.com.au; levels 1 & 2, 31 Tattersalls Lane, cnr Lonsdale St; ⊗noon-1am; 🛜; 🚉Melbourne Central) Run by same folk as Section 8 next door, this dive bar/art space is set over several levels. Within its gritty confines they play everything from electronic to live Polish jazz, while Wednesday nights they project computer games on the opposing giant brick wall. They also sell hot dogs.

Robot
BAR

(Map p58; ☑03-9620 3646; www.robotsushi.com; 12 Bligh Pl; ⊗5pm-late Mon-Fri, 8pm-late Sat; 🚉Flinders St) If neo-Tokyo is your thing, or you just have a sudden urge for a sushi handroll washed down with an Asahi, check out Robot. It has an all-welcome door policy, big windows that open to the laneway, a cute mezzanine level and attracts a laid-back young crowd.

Ponyfish Island
CAFE, BAR

(Map p58; www.ponyfish.com.au; under Yarra Pedestrian Bridge; ⊗8am-1am; 🚉Flinders St) Laneway bars have been done to death; now Melburnians are finding new creative spots to do their drinkin'. Where better than an open-air nook under a bridge arcing over the Yarra? From Flinders St Station underground passage, head over the pedestrian bridge towards Southgate, where you'll find steps down to people knocking back beers with toasted sangas or cheese plates.

Young & Jackson's
PUB

(Map p58; www.youngandjacksons.com.au; cnr Flinders & Swanston Sts; ⊗11am-late; 🚉Flinders St) Opposite Flinders St station, this historic pub has been serving up beer since 1861 and makes for a popular meeting spot. Lounge on chesterfields in Chloe's Bar, or head up to the rooftop cider bar, where nine Australian ciders are on tap, including the house-brewed speciality.

Alumbra

CLUB

(☑03-8623 9666; www.alumbra.com.au; Shed 9, Central Pier, 161 Harbour Esplanade; ◷4pm-3am Fri & Sat, to 1am Sun; ⊟Tourist Shuttle, ⊟70, City Circle) Great music and a stunning location will impress – even if the Bali-meets-Morocco follies of the decor don't. If you're going to do one megaclub in Melbourne (and like the idea of a glass dance floor), this is going to be your best bet. It's in one of the old sheds jutting out into Docklands' Victoria Harbour.

🍺 Fitzroy & Around

Naked for Satan

BAR

(☑03-9416 2238; www.nakedforsatan.com.au; 285 Brunswick St, Fitzroy; ◷noon-midnight Sun-Thu, to 1am Fri & Sat; ⊟112) Vibrant, loud and reviving an apparent Brunswick St legend (a man nicknamed Satan who would get down and dirty, naked because of the heat, in an illegal vodka distillery under the shop), this place packs a punch both with its popular *pintxos* (Basque tapas; $2), huge range of cleverly named beverages and unbeatable roof terrace with wraparound decked balcony.

Everleigh

COCKTAIL BAR

(www.theeverleigh.com; 150-156 Gertrude St, Fitzroy; ◷5.30pm-1am; ⊟86) Sophistication and bartending standards are off the charts at this upstairs hidden nook. Settle into a leather booth in the intimate setting with a few friends for conversation and oohing and ahhing over classic 'golden era' cocktails like you've never tasted before.

Wesley Anne

BAR

(☑03-9482 1333; www.wesleyanne.com.au; 250 High St, Northcote; ◷noon-late; ⊟86, ⊟Northcote) This atmospheric pub set up shop in a church mission's house of assembly. What else can you expect when the demon drink wins out against the forces of temperance? Booze, yes, but also interesting food, live music, a big beer garden with space heaters and a cruisy crowd who often bring their kids along in daylight hours.

Panama Dining Room

BAR

(☑03-9417 7663; www.thepanama.com.au; 3rd fl, 231 Smith St, Fitzroy; ◷5-11pm Sun-Wed, to midnight Thu, to 1am Fri & Sat; ⊟86) Gawp at the ersatz Manhattan views in this large warehouse-style space while sipping serious cocktails and snacking on truffled polenta chips or falafel balls with tahini. The dining area gets packed around 9pm for its Mod European menu.

Industry Beans

CAFE

(www.industrybeans.com; cnr Fitzroy & Rose Sts, Fitzroy; ◷7am-4pm Mon-Fri, 8am-5pm Sat & Sun; ☏; ⊟96, 112) It's all about coffee chemistry at this warehouse cafe tucked in a Fitzroy side street. The coffee guide takes you through the speciality styles on offer (roasted on site) and helpful staff take the pressure off deciding. Pair your brew with some latte coffee pearls or coffee toffee prepared in the 'lab'. The food menu is ambitious, but doesn't always hit the mark.

Napier Hotel

PUB

(☑03-9419 4240; www.thenapierhotel.com; 210 Napier St, Fitzroy; ◷3-11pm Mon-Thu, 1pm-1am Fri & Sat, 1-11pm Sun; ⊟86, 112) The Napier has stood on this corner for over a century – many pots have been pulled as the face of the neighbourhood changed, as demonstrated by the memorabilia of the sadly departed Fitzroy footy team. Worm your way around the central bar to the boisterous dining room for an iconic Bogan Burger. Head upstairs to check out its gallery, too.

Rose

PUB

(406 Napier St, Fitzroy; ◷noon-midnight Sun-Wed, to 1am Thu-Sat; ⊟86, 112) A much-loved Fitzroy backstreet local, the Rose has remained true to its roots with cheap counter meals and a non-pretentious crowd here to watch the footy.

Melbourne Supper Club (p71)
GREG ELMS/GETTY IMAGES ©

Little Creatures Dining Hall   BEER HALL
(☑03-9417 5500;   www.littlecreatures.com.au;
222 Brunswick St, Fitzroy; ⊘8am-late; ☎; 🖂112)
This vast drinking hall is the perfect place
to imbibe from one of Australia's most suc-
cessful microbreweries and gorge on pizzas.
Also has free use of community bikes with
picnic baskets, so pick up one of its beery
hampers.

Carlton & Around

Seven Seeds   CAFE
(www.sevenseeds.com.au; 114 Berkeley St, Carlton; ⊘7am-5pm Mon-Sat, 8am-5pm Sun; 🖂19,
59) The most spacious of the Seven Seeds
coffee empire – there's plenty of room to
store your bike and sip a splendid coffee
beside the other lucky people who've found
this rather out-of-the-way warehouse cafe.
Public cuppings (coffee tastings) are held
Wednesday (9am) and Saturday (10am).

Jimmy Watson's   WINE BAR
(☑03-9347 3985; www.jimmywatsons.com.au; 333
Lygon St, Carlton; ⊘11am-11pm; 🖂1, 8) Keep it
tidy at Watson's wine bar with something
nice by the glass, or go a bottle of dry and
dry (vermouth and ginger ale) and settle in
for the afternoon and evening. If this Robyn
Boyd–designed stunning mid-century building had ears, there'd be a few generations of
writers, students and academics in trouble.

Alderman   WINE BAR
(134 Lygon St, East Brunswick; ⊘5pm-late Tue-Fri,
2pm-late Sat & Sun; ☎; 🖂1, 8) A classic East
Brunswick local, the Alderman has an in-
viting, traditional, heavy wooden bar, open
fireplace, good beer selection and cocktails by
the jug. There's a small courtyard and you can
order from restaurant Bar Idda next door.

Brunswick East Project   CAFE
(☑03-9381 1881; www.padrecoffee.com.au; 438
Lygon St, East Brunswick; ⊘7am-4pm Mon-Sat,
8am-4pm Sun; 🖂1, 8) Another big player in
Melbourne's coffee movement, this East
Brunswick warehouse-style cafe is the original roaster for Padre Coffee and brews its
premium single-origins and blends. Also
has **League of Honest Coffee** (Map p58; 8
Exploration Lane; ⊘7am-5pm Mon-Fri; 🖂City Circle, 24, 30) and stalls at the **Queen Victoria
Market** (String Bean Alley, M Shed near Peel St;
⊘7am-2pm Tue & Thu, to 4pm Fri-Sun; 🖂55) and
South Melbourne Market (www.padrecoffee.
com.au; shop 33; ⊘7am-4pm Wed, Sat & Sun, to
5pm Fri; 🖂96).

Brunswick Green   BAR
(313 Sydney Rd, Brunswick; ⊘4pm-midnight Tue-Thu,
2pm-1am Fri & Sat, 2-11pm Sun; 🖂19, 🚉 Brunswick)
A cool Brunswick local with bohemian front
bar, comfy share-house-style lounge and backyard beer garden. Wednesday nights feature
the popular Variety Collective performers.

South Melbourne

Clement   CAFE
(www.clementcoffee.com; South Melbourne Market,
116-136 Cecil St, South Melbourne; ⊘7am-5pm;
🖂96) There's a buzz about this tiny cafe on
the perimeter of the South Melbourne Market, not only for its expertly crafted brew but
also for the homemade salted-caramel or jam-
and-custard donuts. Grab a streetside stool or
takeaway and wander the market.

Eve   CLUB
(☑03-9696 7388; www.evebar.com.au; 334 City Rd,
South Melbourne; ⊘dusk-late Thu-Sat; 🖂112) Flor-
ence Broadhurst wallpaper, a black granite
bar and Louis chairs set the tone, which gets
rapidly lower as the night progresses. Foot-
ballers, glamour girls and the odd lost soul
come for cocktails and commercial house.
Expect to queue after 9pm.

☆ Entertainment

**Australian Centre for the
Moving Image**   CINEMA
(ACMI; Map p58; ☑03-9663 2583; www.acmi.net.
au; Federation Sq; 🖂1, 48, 70, 72, 75, 🚉 Flinders St)
ACMI's cinemas screen a diverse range of
films. It programs regular events and festivals for film genres and audiences, as well as
screening one-offs.

Rooftop Cinema   CINEMA
(Map p58; www.rooftopcinema.com.au; level 6, Curtin House, 252 Swanston St; 🚉 Melbourne Central)
This rooftop bar sits at dizzying heights on
top of the happening Curtin House. In summer it transforms into an outdoor cinema
with striped deckchairs and a calendar of
new and classic flicks.

Moonlight Cinema   CINEMA
(www.moonlight.com.au; Gate D, Birdwood Ave, Royal Botanic Gardens; 🖂8) Melbourne's original
outdoor cinema, with the option of 'Gold
Grass' tickets that include a glass of wine and
a reserved bean-bag bed.

La Mama   THEATRE
(☑03-9347 6948; www.lamama.com.au; 205 Fara-
day St, Carlton; 🖂1, 8) La Mama is historically

significant in Melbourne's theatre scene. This tiny, intimate forum produces new Australian works and experimental theatre, and has a reputation for developing emerging playwrights. It's a ramshackle building with an open-air bar. Shows also run at its larger **Courthouse Theater** (349 Drummond St), so check tickets carefully for the correct location.

Malthouse Theatre
THEATRE

(☑03-9685 5111; www.malthousetheatre.com.au; 113 Sturt St, Southbank; ☺1) The Malthouse Theatre Company often produces the most exciting theatre in Melbourne. Dedicated to promoting Australian works, the company has been housed in the atmospheric Malthouse Theatre since 1990 (when it was known as the Playbox). From Flinders St Station walk across Princes Bridge and along St Kilda Rd. Turn right at Grant St, then left into Sturt St.

Melbourne Theatre Company
THEATRE

(MTC; ☑03-8688 0800; www.mtc.com.au; 140 Southbank Blvd, Southbank; ☺1) Melbourne's major theatrical company stages around 15 productions each year, ranging from contemporary and modern (including many new Australian works) to Shakespearean and other classics. Performances take place in a brand-new, award-winning venue in Southbank.

Last Laugh at the Comedy Club
COMEDY

(Map p58; ☑03-9650 1977; www.thecomedyclub.com.au; Athenaeum Theatre, 188 Collins St; show $25; ☺Fri & Sat; ☺1, 72, 112, ☺Flinders St) The Last Laugh is open Friday and Saturday night year-round, with additional evenings in summer. This is professional stand-up, featuring local and international artists. Dinner-show packages ($55) are available – bookings recommended. The club is also a venue for acts during the Comedy Festival.

Live Music

Check daily papers and weekly street magazines **Beat** (www.beat.com.au) and **The Music** (www.themusic.com.au) for gig info. Radio station 3RRR (102.7FM) broadcasts a gig guide at 7pm each evening and puts it online at www.rrr.org.au.

Esplanade Hotel
LIVE MUSIC

(The Espy; ☑03-9534 0211; www.espy.com.au; 11 The Esplanade, St Kilda; ☺noon-1am Sun-Wed, to 3am Thu-Sat; ☺16, 96) Rock pigs rejoice. The Espy remains gloriously shabby and welcoming to all. A mix of local and international bands play nightly, everything from rock 'n' roll to hip hop, either in the legendary Gershwin Room, the front bar or down in the basement.

The Tote
LIVE MUSIC

(☑03-9419 5320; www.thetotehotel.com; cnr Johnston & Wellington Sts, Collingwood; ☺4pm-late Tue-Sun; ☺86) One of Melbourne's most iconic live-music venues, not only does this divey Collingwood pub have a great roster of local and international underground bands, but one of the best jukeboxes in the universe. Its temporary closure in 2010 brought Melbourne to a stop, literally – people protested on the streets against the liquor licensing laws blamed for the closure.

Corner Hotel
LIVE MUSIC

(☑03-9427 9198; www.cornerhotel.com; 57 Swan St, Richmond; ☺4pm-late Tue & Wed, noon-late Thu-Sun; ☺70, ☺Richmond) The band room here is one of Melbourne's most popular midsized venues and has seen plenty of loud and live action over the years, from Dinosaur Jr to the Buzzcocks. If your ears need a break, there's a friendly front bar. The rooftop has city views, but gets super-packed, often with a different crowd from the music fans below.

Northcote Social Club
LIVE MUSIC

(☑03-9489 3917; www.northcotesocialclub.com; 301 High St, Northcote; ☺4pm-late Mon & Tue, noon-late Wed-Sun; ☺86, ☺Northcote) The stage at this inner-north local has seen plenty of international folk just one album out from star status. Its home-grown line-up is also notable. If you're just after a drink, the front bar buzzes every night of the week, and there's a large deck out back for lazy afternoons.

Cherry
LIVE MUSIC

(Map p58; www.cherrybar.com.au; AC/DC Lane; ☺6pm-3am Tue & Wed, 5pm-5am Thu-Sat, 2-6.30pm Sun; ☺City Circle, 70, 75) Melbourne's legendary rock 'n' roll bar is still going strong. Located down AC/DC Lane (yep, named after the band, who are home-grown heroes), there's often a queue, but once inside, a welcoming, slightly anarchic spirit prevails. Live music and DJs play rock 'n' roll seven nights a week, and there's a long-standing soul night on Thursdays. It's the choice of touring bands to hang out post-gig – the bar made headlines by knocking back Lady Gaga to honour a local band's booking.

Old Bar
LIVE MUSIC

(☑03-9417 4155; www.theoldbar.com.au; 74-76 Johnston St, Fitzroy; ☺; ☺96, 112) With live bands seven days a week and a license till 3am, the Old Bar's another reason why Melbourne is the rock 'n' roll capital of Australia. It gets great local bands and a few internationals playing in its grungy bandroom with a house-party vibe.

Evelyn Hotel
LIVE MUSIC

(☑ 03-9419 5500; www.evelynhotel.com; 351 Brunswick St, Fitzroy; ⊙ 12.30pm-1.30am; 🚊 112) Playing mostly local acts, the Evelyn also pulls the occasional international performer. The Ev doesn't discriminate by genre: if it's quality, it gets a look in here.

Palais Theatre
CONCERT VENUE

(☑ 03-9525 3240, tickets 13 61 00; www.palaistheatre.net.au; Lower Esplanade, St Kilda; 🚊 3a, 16, 79, 96) Standing gracefully next to Luna Park, the heritage-listed Palais (c 1927) is a St Kilda icon. Not only is the theatre a beautiful old space, but it also stages some pretty special performances, from international bands to big-name comedians.

Dance, Classical Music & Opera

Australian Ballet
BALLET

(☑ 1300 369 741; www.australianballet.com.au; 2 Kavanagh St; 🚊 1) Based in Melbourne and now more than 40 years old, the Australian Ballet performs traditional and new works at the State Theatre in the Arts Centre. You can take an hour-long Australian Ballet Centre tour ($18, bookings essential) that includes a visit to the production and wardrobe departments as well as the studios of both the company and the school.

Hamer Hall
CONCERT VENUE

(Melbourne Concert Hall; Map p58; ☑ 1300 182 183; www.artscentremelbourne.com.au; Arts Centre Melbourne, 100 St Kilda Rd; 🚊 1, 3, 16, 64, 72, 🚊 Flinders St) After a multimillion-dollar redevelopment, the concert hall is well known for its excellent acoustics, with a decor inspired by Australia's mineral and gemstone deposits.

Melbourne Symphony Orchestra
ORCHESTRA

(MSO; Map p58; ☑ 03-9929 9600; www.mso.com.au) The MSO has a broad reach – while not afraid to be populist (it's done sell-out performances with both Burt Bacharach and the Whitlams), it can also do edgy – such as performing with Kiss – along with its performances of the great masterworks of symphony.

Opera Australia
OPERA

(☑ 03-9685 3700; www.opera.org.au; cnr Fawkner & Fanning Sts, Southbank) The national opera company performs with some regularity at Melbourne's Victorian Arts Centre.

Sport

Melbourne is a sport-obsessed city. From March to October it's all about AFL footy, while rugby league, soccer and union are also very popular. In summer, cricket dominates.

Melbourne Cricket Ground
SPECTATOR SPORT

(☑ 03-9657 8888; www.mcg.org.au) Melbourne's sporting mecca, the MCG (p61), or 'G', hosts cricket in the summer and AFL footy in the winter. Attendance is a rite of passage for many locals.

Melbourne Park
SPECTATOR SPORT

(☑ 03-9286 1600; www.mopt.com.au; Batman Ave, Richmond; tours adult/child/family $15/7/35; 🚊 48, 70, 75, 🚊 Jolimont) Home to the **Australian Open Tennis** grand slam in January, Melbourne Park precinct has 34 courts, including its centrepiece **Rod Laver Arena**. You can take a tour to the dressing rooms, VIP areas and super-boxes. Its indoor-court hire ranges from $36 to $42, and outdoor courts cost between $28 and $36, plus racquet hire.

Flemington Racecourse
HORSE RACING

(☑ 1300 727 575; www.vrc.net.au; 400 Epsom Rd, Flemington; 🚊 57, 🚊 Flemington Racecourse) Home of the Victoria Racing Club, Flemington has regular horse-race meets, climaxing with the Spring Racing Carnival (including the Melbourne Cup; p66) from October to November.

🛍 Shopping

Melbourne is a city of passionate, dedicated retailers catering to a broad range of tastes, whims and lifestyles. From boutique-filled city lanes to suburban shopping streets and malls, you'll find plenty of places to offload your cash and pick up something unique.

🛍 Central Melbourne

Melbourne's city centre has everything from boutiques hidden in lanes to large shopping complexes such as QV, Emporium and Melbourne Central with major international brands.

★ Craft Victoria Shop
CRAFTS

(Craft Victoria; Map p58; ☑ 03-9650 7775; www.craft.org.au; 31 Flinders Lane; ⊙ 11am-6pm Mon-Sat; 🚊 City Circle, 70, 75) This retail arm of Craft Victoria showcases the best of handmade crafts, mainly from local Victorian artists. Its range of jewellery, textiles, accessories, glass and ceramics bridges the art/craft divide and makes for some wonderful mementos of Melbourne. There are also a few galleries with changing exhibitions; admission is free.

Somewhere FASHION, ACCESSORIES
(Map p58; www.someplace.com.au; Royal Arcade, 2/314 Little Collins St; ⊙10am-6pm Mon-Thu & Sat, to 8pm Fri, 11am-5pm Sun; ⊞86, 96) Somewhere is an apt name for this hard-to-find treasure. It's located at the Little Collins St end of Royal Arcade (look for the Marais sign and take the stairs to level 2). The white-washed warehouse space stocks predominantly Scandinavian labels, as well as local designers, along with leather tote bags, Anne Black ceramic jewellery and a good range of denim.

Incu FASHION
(Map p58; ☑03-9663 9933; www.incuclothing.com; shop 6a, 274 Flinders Lane; ⊙10am-6pm Mon-Thu & Sat, to 8pm Fri, 11am-5pm Sun; ⊞Flinders St) Sydney retailer Incu has set up store in Melbourne and stocks a range of contemporary designers for menswear, with crisp tailored shirts from Weathered, comfy chinos and great stuff from labels such as Vanishing Elephant and Kloke. Its women's store is in the QV Building.

Captains of Industry CLOTHING, ACCESSORIES
(Map p58; ☑03-9670 4405; www.captainsofindustry.com.au; level 1, 2 Somerset Pl; ⊙9am-5pm; ⊞19, 57, 59) Where can you get a haircut, a bespoke suit and a pair of shoes or a leather wallet made in the one place? Here. The hard-working folk at spacious and industrial Captains also offer homey breakfasts and lunches, and it turns into a low-key bar on Friday nights.

RM Williams CLOTHING
(Map p58; ☑03-9663 7126; www.rmwilliams.com.au; Melbourne Central, Lonsdale St; ⊙10am-6pm Mon-Thu & Sat, to 9pm Fri, to 5pm Sun) An Aussie icon, even for city slickers, this brand will kit you up with stylish essentials for working the land, including a pair of those famous boots.

Original & Authentic Aboriginal Art ARTS, CRAFTS
(Map p58; ☑03-9663 5133; www.originaland authenticaboriginalart.com; 90 Bourke St; ⊙11am-6pm; ⊞86, 96) Open for 25 years this centrally located gallery has a good relationship with its Indigenous artists across Australia and offers stunning and affordable pieces, all with author profiles.

NGV Shop at the Ian Potter Centre BOOKS, GIFTS
(Map p58; www.ngv.vic.gov.au; Federation Sq; ⊞Flinders St) This gallery shop has a wide range of international design magazines, a kids' section and the usual gallery standards. Also at NGV International (p57).

Melbournalia GIFTS, SOUVENIRS
(Map p58; www.melbournalia.com.au; shop 5, 50 Bourke St; ⊙10am-6pm Mon-Thu, to 8pm Fri, 11am-5pm Sat & Sun; ⊞86, 96) Pop-up store turned permanent, this is the place to stock up on interesting souvenirs by local designers – from tram tote bags and city-rooftop honey to prints of the city's icons and great books on Melbourne.

🔖 Fitzroy & Around

Gertrude St has become one of Melbourne's most interesting shopping strips. Smith St is decidedly vintage, with small boutique stores, though its northern end, beyond Johnston St, is jam-packed with clearance stores. Brunswick St is a mixed bag, but it does have some good boutique designers between Johnston and Gertrude St.

★**Third Drawer Down** HOMEWARES
(www.thirddrawerdown.com; 93 George St, Fitzroy; ⊙11am-5pm Mon-Sat; ⊞86) It all started with its signature tea-towel designs (now found in MOMA in New York) at this 'museum of art souvenirs'. Third Drawer Down makes life beautifully unusual by stocking absurdist pieces with a sense of humour, as well as high-end art by well-known designers.

Mud Australia CERAMICS
(☑03-9419 5161; www.mudaustralia.com; 181 Gertrude St, Fitzroy; ⊙10am-6pm Mon-Fri, to 5pm Sat, noon-5pm Sun; ⊞86) You'll find some of the most aesthetically beautiful – as well as functional – porcelain from Australian-designed Mud. Coffee mugs, milk pourers, salad bowls and serving plates come in muted pastel colours with a raw matt finish. Prices start from $20 per piece.

Crumpler ACCESSORIES
(☑03-9417 5338; www.crumpler.com; 87 Smith St, cnr Gertrude St, Fitzroy; ⊙10am-6pm Mon-Sat, to 5pm Sun; ⊞86) Crumpler's bike-courier bags, designed by two former couriers looking for a bag they could hold their beer in while cycling home, started it all. Its durable, practical designs now extend to bags for cameras, laptops and iPods, and can be found around the world.

Gorman
CLOTHING, ACCESSORIES

(www.gormanshop.com.au; 235 Brunswick St, Fitzroy; ⊙10am-6pm Mon-Thu & Sat, to 7pm Fri, 11am-5pm Sun; 🚊112) Lisa Gorman makes everyday clothes that are far from ordinary: boyish, but sexy short shapes are cut from exquisite fabrics, and pretty cardigans are coupled with relaxed, organic tees. You can find other branches in the GPO (☑03-9663 0066; www.melbournesgpo.com; cnr Elizabeth St & Bourke St Mall; ⊙10am-6pm Mon-Thu & Sat, to 8pm Fri, 11am-5pm Sun; 🚊19, 57, 59, 86, 96) and elsewhere around town.

Aesop
BEAUTY

(☑03-9419 8356; www.aesop.com; 242 Gertrude St, Fitzroy; ⊙11am-5pm Mon & Sun, 10am-6pm Tue-Fri, to 5pm Sat; 🚊86) This home-grown empire specialises in citrus-and-botanical-based aromatic balms, hair masques, scents, cleansers and oils in beautifully simple packaging for both men and women. There are plenty of branches around town (and plenty of opportunity to sample the products in most of Melbourne's cafe bathrooms).

🔒 Carlton & Around

Readings
BOOKS

(www.readings.com.au; 309 Lygon St, Carlton; ⊙8am-11pm Mon-Fri, 9am-11pm Sat, to 9pm Sun; 🚊Tourist Shuttle, 🚊1, 8) A potter around this defiantly prospering indie bookshop can occupy an entire afternoon if you're so inclined. There's a dangerously loaded (and good-value) specials table, switched-on staff and everyone from Lacan to *Charlie & Lola* on the shelves. Its exterior housemate-wanted board is legendary. Also in St Kilda (☑03-9525 3852; www.readings.com.au; 112 Acland St; 🚊96) and the city centre (State Library, cnr La Trobe & Swanston Sts; 🚊Melbourne Central).

Gewürzhaus
FOOD

(www.gewurzhaus.com.au; 342 Lygon St, Carlton; ⊙10am-6pm Mon-Sat, 11am-5pm Sun; 🚊1, 8) Set up by two enterprising young German girls, this store is a chef's dream with its displays of spices from around the world, including Indigenous Australian blends, flavoured salts and sugars. It has high-quality cooking accessories and gifts, and cooking classes, too. There's a city store inside the Block Arcade (282 Collins St; 🚊19, 57, 59).

Block Arcade

Great Ocean Road

The Great Ocean Road is one of Australia's most famous road-touring routes. Hunt out the isolated beaches and lighthouses in between the towns, and the thick eucalypt forests in the Otway hinterlands to really escape the crowds.

Torquay

POP 13,339

In the 1960s and '70s Torquay was just another sleepy seaside town. Back then, surfing in Australia was a decidedly counter-cultural pursuit, its devotees crusty hippy dropouts living in clapped-out Kombis, smoking pot and making off with your daughters. Nowadays there is a lot less counter culture, while the town's proximity to world-renowned Bells Beach and its status as home of Rip Curl and Quicksilver both initially wetsuit makers, means Torquay is the undisputed capital of the Australian surf industry.

◉ Sights & Activities

Torquay's beaches lure in all, and there is a spot to suit everyone from toddlers paddling on the water's edge to surfer dudes.

And don't forget about visiting the famous surf beaches nearby, including Jan Juc, Winki Pop and, of course, Bells Beach (p80).

Surf World Museum   MUSEUM
(www.surfworld.com.au; Surf City Plaza; adult/child/family $12/8/30; ◷9am-5pm) The perfect starting point for those embarking on a surfing safari, this well-curated museum pays homage to Australian surfing, from Simon Anderson's ground-breaking 1981 thruster to Mark Richard's board collection and, most notably, Australia's Surfing Hall of Fame. It's full of great memorabilia (including Duke Kahanamoku's wooden longboard), videos and displays on surfing culture through the 1960s to '80s.

Go Ride a Wave   SURFING
(☑1300 132 441; www.gorideawave.com.au; 1/15 Bell St; 2hr lesson incl hire $65) Hires surfing gear, sells second-hand equipment and offers lessons (cheaper with advance booking).

ⓘ ORGANISED TOURS

Go West Tours (☑1300 736 551; www.gowest.com.au; tour $125) Full-day tours visit Bells Beach, koalas in the Otways and Port Campbell, returning back to Melbourne. Free wi-fi on bus.

Otway Discovery Tour (☑03-9629 5844; www.greatoceanroadtour.com.au; 1-/2-/3-day tour $99/249/355) Very affordable Great Ocean Road tours. The two-day tours visit Phillip Island, while the three-day version takes in the Grampians.

Ride Tours (☑1800 605 120; www.ridetours.com.au; tour $210) Two-day, one-night trips along the Great Ocean Road.

Great Ocean Road Surf Tours (☑1800 787 353; www.gorsurftours.com.au; 106 Surf Coast Hwy) Multiday surf trips down the coast from $309, including accommodation in Torquay.

BELLS BEACH, POINT ADDIS & HISTORIC MARKERS

Work on the Great Ocean Road began in September 1919. It involved more than 3000 workers, mostly returned WWI soldiers, with initial construction done by hand, using picks, shovels and crowbars. A slight detour off the B100 takes you to famous **Bells Beach**, the point break that is part of international surfing folklore. When the long right hander is working, it's one of the longest rides in the country.

Since 1973, Bells has hosted the **Rip Curl Pro** (www.aspworldtour.com) every Easter. The world championship ASP tour event draws thousands to watch the world's best surfers carve up the big autumn swells – waves have reached 5m during the contest! The Rip Curl Pro occasionally decamps to Johanna Beach, two hours west, when fickle Bells isn't working.

Nine kilometres southwest of Torquay is the turn-off to spectacular **Point Addis**, a vast sweep of pristine clothing-optional beach that attracts surfers, nudists, hang-gliders and swimmers. The signposted **Koorie Cultural Walk** is a 1km circuit trail to the beach through the **Ironbark Basin** nature reserve.

Between Torquay to Lavers Hill, keep an eye out for 13 bronze plaques that tell the story of the road'ss construction, most with spectacular views that are great photo ops. At Eastern View (just after Fairhaven en route to Lorne) you'll find the Diggers sculpture, which sits beneath the historic Memorial Arch and depicts an ex-WWI soldier labourer. For further info on its construction visit the **Great Ocean Road National Heritage Centre** (p21) in Lorne.

Torquay Surfing Academy SURFING
See p20.

Westcoast Surf School SURFING
See p20.

🛏 Sleeping

Bells Beach Backpackers HOSTEL **$**
(☑03-5261 4029; www.bellsbeachbackpackers.com.au; 51-53 Surfcoast Hwy; dm/d from $26/80; @🛜) On the main highway, this friendly backpackers does a great job of fitting into the fabric of this surf town, with board hire, daily surf reports and a good collection of surf videos. Its basic rooms are clean and in good nick.

Woolshed B&B B&B **$$$**
(☑0408 333 433; www.thewoolshedtorquay.com.au; 75 Aquarius Ave; apt incl breakfast $275; ✳✳) Set on a gorgeous farm on Torquay's outskirts, this century-old woolshed has been converted into a gorgeous open and airy space with two bedrooms. It sleeps up to six, and guests can use the pool and tennis court. Book well in advance.

🍴 Eating & Drinking

Cafe Moby CAFE **$**
(☑03-5261 2339; www.cafemoby.com; 41 Esplanade; mains $12-18; ☺7am-4pm; 🛜) This old weatherboard house on the Esplanade harks back to a time when Torquay was simple,

which is not to say its meals aren't modern: fill up on a linguini or honey-roasted lamb souvlaki. There's a whopping great playground out the back for kids.

Bottle of Milk BURGERS, BAR **$**
(☑0456 748 617; www.thebottleofmilk.com; 24 Bell St; burgers from $10; ☺10.30am-late) Trading off the success of its Lorne (p82) branch, Bottle of Milk's winning formula of burgers, beaches and beers makes it rightfully popular. There's a beer garden, too, and excellent coffee.

🛍 Shopping

A smorgasbord of surf shops lines Torquay's main thoroughfare, from big brands to local board shapers. For bargains head down Baines Cres alongside Surf City Plaza for discount surf seconds.

ℹ Information

Torquay Visitor Information Centre (www.greatoceanroad.org; Surf City Plaza, Beach Rd; ☺9am-5pm) Torquay has a well-resourced tourist office next to Surf World Museum. There's free wi-fi and internet available at the library next door.

ℹ Getting There & Away

Torquay is 15 minutes' drive south of Geelong on the B100.

Anglesea

POP 2454

The Great Ocean Road officially begins on the stretch of road between Torquay and Anglesea. It is a popular, and for many families, traditional seaside town in whihc to spend the school holidays, The new Geelong bypass has reduced the time it takes to drive from Melbourne to Anglesea to around 75 minutes.

◉ Sights & Activities

Main Beach is the ideal spot to learn to surf, while sheltered Point Roadknight Beach is good for families. The Anglesea heathlands have a huge diversity of flora and fauna, particularly the wild orchids, with around 100 varieties found around September.

Anglesea Golf Club　　　GOLF
See p20.

Go Ride a Wave　　　SURFING
(☑ 1300 132 441; www.gorideawave.com.au; 143b Great Ocean Rd; 2hr lessons from $65, board hire from $25; ⊗ 9am-5pm) Long-established surf school that runs lessons and hires out boards, SUPs and kayaks.

⛌ Sleeping

Anglesea Backpackers　　　HOSTEL $
(☑ 03-5263 2664; www.angleseabackpackers.com; 40 Noble St; dm from $35, d $95-115, f $150; @) While most hostels like to cram 'em in, this simple, homely backpackers has just two dorm rooms and one double/triple, and is clean, bright and welcoming. In winter the fire glows warmly in the cosy living room.

Anglesea Rivergums　　　B&B $$
(☑ 03-5263 3066; www.anglesearivergums.com.au; 10 Bingley Pde; d $125-160; ❄) Tucked in by the river with tranquil views, these two spacious, tastefully furnished rooms (there's a self-contained bungalow and a room attached to the house) are excellent value.

✕ Eating

★ Uber Mama　　　MODERN AUSTRALIAN $$
(☑ 03-5263 1717; www.ubermama.com.au; 113 Great Ocean Rd; mains $19-33; ⊗ noon-3pm & 6-9pm Thu-Sat, 9am-3pm Sun) An example of the subtle revolution sweeping the kitchens of regional Australia, Uber Mama does modern Aussie cooking with Asian inflections that's creative without straying too far from local roots. Try the shared plates

such as baked Otway brie or seared scallops with prosciutto, or classic fish and chips for a main.

Locanda Del Mare　　　ITALIAN $$
(☑ 03-5263 2904; 5 Diggers Pde; mains $19.50-25; ⊗ from 6pm Thu-Mon summer, from 6pm Tue-Sun winter) Don't be deceived by its ugly exterior; this authentic Italian restaurant, hidden behind Anglesea's petrol station, gets rave reviews, especially for its wonderful desserts.

❶ Information

Anglesea Visitor Information Centre (Great Ocean Rd; ⊗ 9am-5pm) Located opposite Angahook Cafe, this new information centre sits beside an equally new BBQ area.

Lorne

POP 1046

Lorne has an incredible natural beauty, that has attracted visitors for generations. Rudyard Kipling's 1891 visit led him to pen the poem 'Flowers': 'Gathered where the Erskine leaps/Down the road to Lorne...'

It gets busy; in summer you'll be competing with day trippers for restaurant seats and lattes, but, thronged by tourists or not, it's a lovely place to hang out.

◉ Sights & Activities

Kids will really enjoy the beachside swimming pool, trampolines and skate park, while there's more than 50km of bushwalking

---

WORTH A TRIP

BELLARINE FOODIE DETOUR

The Bellarine Peninsula has a growing reputation as a gourmet food region, with a particular focus on wines. With over 50 wineries in the Bellarine and Geelong area, it's known for its cool-climate pinot, shiraz and chardonnay. You could easily spend a lazy couple of days exploring the region. For a list of wineries, check out www.winegeelong.com.au, while visitor centres across the region can help you with suggestions.

Bellarine Taste Trail (www.thebellarine tastetrail.com.au) Combine a winery hop with the Bellarine Taste Trail, which builds itineraries around mostly artisan gourmet-food producers, and you've got yourself a fantastic day out.

tracks nearby, taking in lush forests and waterfalls. Pick up the *Lorne Walks & Waterfalls* brochure from the visitor centre.

Erskine Falls
WATERFALL
See p21.

Great Ocean Road National Heritage Centre
MUSEUM
See p21.

Southern Exposure
WATER SPORTS
(☑ 03-5261 9170; www.southernexposure.com.au; 2hr surf lesson $75) Offers surfing lessons, and is big on kayaking and mountain biking.

★ Festivals & Events

Falls Festival
MUSIC
See p21.

Pier to Pub Swim
SPORTS
(www.lornesurfclub.com.au) This popular event in January inspires up to 4500 swimmers to splash 1.2km across Loutit Bay to the Lorne Hotel. It's a photo opportunity for local politicians and celebrities.

🛏 Sleeping

Great Ocean Road Backpackers
HOSTEL $
(☑ 03-5289 1070; http://greatoceanroadcottages. com; 10 Erskine Ave; dm/d $35/90; ❋ ☎) Tucked away in the bush among the cockatoos, koalas and other wildlife, this two-storey timber lodge has dorms and good-value doubles.

Unisex bathrooms take some getting used to. Also has pricier A-frame cottages that come with kitchens and en suite.

Grand Pacific Hotel
HOTEL $$
(☑ 03-5289 1609; www.grandpacific.com.au; 268 Mountjoy Pde; d/apt from $130/180; ☎) An iconic Lorne landmark, harking back to 1875, the Grand Pacific has been restored with a sleek modern decor that retains some classic period features. The best rooms have balconies and stunning sea views looking out to the pier. Plainer rooms are boxy, but still top value, and there are self-contained apartments, too.

Qdos
RYOKAN $$$
(☑ 03-5289 1989; www.qdosarts.com; 35 Allenvale Rd; r incl breakfast from $250; ☎) The perfect choice for those seeking a romantic getaway or forest retreat, Qdos' luxury Zen treehouses are fitted with tatami mats, rice-paper screens and no TV. Two-night minimum; no kids.

✕ Eating

Bottle of Milk
BURGERS $
(☑ 03-5289 2005; www.thebottleofmilk.com; 52 Mountjoy Pde; burgers from $12; ⊙ 8am-3pm Mon-Fri, to 5pm Sat & Sun Mar-Oct, 8am-9pm daily Nov-Feb) With a menu of 24 inventive burgers, all stacked with fresh ingredients, it's hard to go wrong at this popular hang-out on the main strip.

Falls Festival

Lorne Beach Pavilion   MODERN AUSTRALIAN **$$**
(☑03-5289 2882; www.lornebeachpavilion.com.
au; 81 Mountjoy Pde; breakfast & lunch mains $9-
20, dinner $25-37; ⊙8am-9pm) With its un-
beatable spot on the foreshore, life here is
literally a beach, especially with a cold beer
in hand. Come at happy hour for 1kg of
mussels for $10 and two-for-one cocktails.
Cafe-style breakfasts and lunches are tasty,
while a more upmarket Modern Australian
menu is on for dinner.

Arab   CAFE **$$**
(☑03-5289 1435; 94 Mountjoy Pde; mains $19-26;
⊙7am-8pm Mon-Fri, to 9.30pm Sat & Sun) Arab
started as a beatnik coffee lounge in 1956,
and single-handedly transformed Lorne
from a daggy family-holiday destination
into a place for groovers and shakers. It's
been trading ever since, and still hits the
spot for coffee and all-day breakfasts.

❶ Information

Lorne Visitor Centre (☑1300 891 152; www.
visitgreatoceanroad.org.au/lorne; 15 Mountjoy
Pde; ⊙9am-5pm; 🛜) Stacks of information
(including walking maps), helpful staff, fishing
licences, bus tickets and accommodation
booking service. Also has internet access and
free wi-fi.

Apollo Bay

POP 1094

One of the larger towns along the Great
Ocean Road, Apollo Bay has a tight-knit
community of fisherfolk, artists, musicians
and sea changers. It's also an ideal base for
exploring magical Cape Otway (p56) and
Otway National Park. It has some of the
best restaurants along the coast and two
lively pubs.

🏃 Activities

Mark's Walking Tours   WALKING TOUR
See p21.

Otway Shipwreck Tours   TOUR
See p21.

Apollo Bay Surf & Kayak   WATER SPORTS
See p21.

🛏 Sleeping

YHA Eco Beach   HOSTEL **$**
(☑03-5237 7899; www.yha.com.au; 5 Pascoe St;
dm from $36.50, d/f $101.50/122; @🛜) 🖉 This
$3-million, architect-designed hostel is an

WHERE TO SEE WILDLIFE

The Great Ocean Road is not just one of
the world's best road trips. It's also one of
the best places in Australia to see wildlife.

Kangaroos

Anglesea Golf Club (p20)
Tower Hill Reserve (15km west of
Warrnambool). Also good for emus and
koalas.

Platypus

Lake Elizabeth (7km from Forrest,
which is a 30-minute drive from Apollo Bay). Contact Otway Eco Tours
(☑0419 670 985; www.platypustours.net.
au; adult/child $85/50).

Koalas

Kennett River (p21)
Cape Otway (p84)

Penguins

Twelve Apostles (p23)
London Bridge (p85)

Southern Right Whales

Warrnambool (May to September; p87)
Portland (May to September)

Black Wallabies

Port Fairy (p87)

outstanding place to stay, with eco creden-
tials, great lounge areas, kitchens, boules pit
and rooftop terraces. Rooms are generic but
spotless. It's a block behind the beach.

Surfside Backpacker   HOSTEL **$**
(☑03-5237 7263; www.surfsidebackpacker.
com; cnr Great Ocean Rd & Gambier St; dm from
$28, d $75; 🛜) Right across from the beach,
this fantastic, sprawling, old-school 1940s
beach house will appeal to those looking
for budget accommodation with character (though possibly not to those seeking
a sleek, modern hostel). Its homely lounge
is full of couches, board games and huge
windows looking out onto the ocean. It's a
15-minute walk from the bus stop.

⭐**Beacon Point**
Ocean View Villas   VILLA **$$**
(☑03-5237 6196; www.beaconpoint.com.au; 270
Skenes Creek Rd; r from $165; ❄) With a com-
manding hill location among the trees,
this wonderful collection of comfortable

one- and two-bedroom villas is a luxurious yet affordable bush retreat. Most villas have sensational coast views, balcony and wood-fired heater.

✕ Eating & Drinking

Bay Leaf Café
CAFE $

(☑ 03-5237 6470; 131 Great Ocean Rd; mains $11-17; ⊘ 8.30am-2.30pm) A local favourite for its innovative menu, good coffee, friendly atmosphere and boutique-beer selection.

Apollo Bay Hotel
PUB $$

(☑ 03-5237 6250; www.apollobayhotel.com.au; 95 Great Ocean Rd; mains $18-36; ⊘ 11am-11pm) This pub's enticing street-front beer garden is the place to be in summer. The bistro has good seafood options and there are live bands on weekends.

★ Chris's Beacon Point Restaurant
GREEK $$$

(☑ 03-5237 6411; www.chriss.com.au; 280 Skenes Creek Rd; mains from $38; ⊘ 8.30-10am & 6pm-late daily, plus noon-2pm Sat & Sun; ☎) Feast on memorable ocean views, deliciously fresh seafood and Greek-influenced dishes at Chris' hilltop fine-dining sanctuary among the treetops. Reservations recommended. You can also stay in its wonderful stilted villas ($265 to $330). It's accessed via Skenes Creek.

ⓘ Information

Great Ocean Road Visitor Centre (☑ 1300 689 297; 100 Great Ocean Rd; ⊘ 9am-5pm; ☎) Modern and professional tourist office with a heap of info for the area, and an 'eco-centre' with displays. It has free wi-fi and can book bus tickets, too.

Cape Otway

The coastline, while particularly beautiful, is rugged and has historically been dangerous to passing ships. The turn-off for Lighthouse Rd, which leads 12km down to the lighthouse, is 21km from Apollo Bay.

◉ Sights & Activities

Cape Otway Lightstation
LIGHTHOUSE

See p21.

⌸ Sleeping

★ Bimbi Park
CARAVAN PARK $

(☑ 03-5237 9246; www.bimbipark.com.au; 90 Manna Gum Dr; unpowered/powered sites $20/30,

dm $45, d cabins $60-185; ☎) ✎ Down a dirt road 3km from the lighthouse is this character-filled caravan park with bush sites, cabins, dorms and old-school caravans. It's good for families, with plenty of wildlife, including koalas, horse rides ($45 per hour) and a rock-climbing wall. Good use of water-saving initiatives.

Cape Otway Lightstation
B&B $$$

(Cape Otway lightstation; ☑ 03-5237 9240; www.lightstation.com; Lighthouse Rd; d from $255) There's a range of options at this wind-swept spot. You can book out the whole Head Lightkeeper's House (sleeps 16), or the smaller Manager's House (sleeps two). Prices are halved if you stay a second night. Vans are also permitted to stay for $25, but you'll need to pay the admission fee.

★ Great Ocean Ecolodge
LODGE $$$

(☑ 03-5237 9297; www.greatoceanecolodge.com; 635 Lighthouse Rd; r incl breakfast & activities from $380; ☞) ✎ Reminiscent of a luxury African safari lodge, this mud-brick homestead stands in pastoral surrounds with plenty of wildlife. It's all solar-powered and rates go towards the on-site Centre for Conservation Ecology (www.conservation ecologycentre.org).

It also serves as an animal hospital for local fauna, and it has a captive tiger quoll breeding program, which you'll visit on its dusk wildlife walk with an ecologist.

Port Campbell National Park

The road levels out after leaving the Otways and continues along a narrow, flat scrubby escarpment that falls away to sheer, 70m-high cliffs between Princetown and Peterborough. The Port Campbell National Park is home to the Twelve Apostles, and is possibly the most famous and photographed stretch of the Great Ocean Road.

Note that this stretch of beach is not suitable for swimming due to the strong currents and an undertows.

◉ Sights & Activities

★ Twelve Apostles
LANDMARK

See p23.

Loch Ard Gorge
BEACH

See p24.

HOW MANY APOSTLES?

The Twelve Apostles are not 12 in number and, from all records, never have been. From the viewing platform you can clearly count seven Apostles, but maybe some obscure others? We consulted widely with Parks Victoria officers, tourist-office staff and even the cleaner at the lookout, but it's still not clear. Locals tend to say 'It depends where you look from', which really is true.

The Apostles are called 'stacks' in geologic parlance, and the rock formations were originally named the 'Sow and Piglets'. Since becoming 'apostles' and because apostles tend to come by the dozen, the number 12 was added sometime later.

The soft limestone cliffs around here are constantly being eroded by the unceasing waves – one 70m-high stack collapsed into the sea in July 2005 and the Island Archway lost its archway in June 2009.

Gibson Steps   BEACH
These 86 steps, hacked by hand into the cliffs by 19th-century landowner Hugh Gibson (and more recently replaced by concrete steps), lead down to wild Gibson Beach. You can walk along the beach, but be careful not to be stranded by high tides.

London Bridge   LANDMARK
Just outside Port Campbell, en route to Peterborough, London Bridge has indeed fallen down. It was once a double-arched rock platform linked to the mainland, until January 1990, when it collapsed, leaving two tourists temporarily maroone. It remains a spectacular sight nevertheless.

12 Apostles Helicopters   HELICOPTER TOUR
See p24.

Port Campbell

POP 260

This small, laid-back coastal town was named after Scottish Captain Alexander Campbell, a whaler who took refuge here on trading voyages between Tasmania and Port Fairy. It's a friendly spot with some great budget-accommodation options, which make for an ideal spot to debrief after visiting the Twelve Apostles. Its tiny bay has a lovely sandy beach, one of the few safe places for swimming along this tempestuous stretch of coast.

Tours

Port Campbell Touring Company   TOUR
(☑03-5598 6424; www.portcampbelltouring.com. au; half-day tours from $100) Runs Apostle Coast tours and walking tours, including a Loch Ard evening walk ($65).

Sleeping

Port Campbell Guesthouse   GUESTHOUSE $
(☑0407 696 559; www.portcampbellguesthouse. com; 54 Lord St; s/d incl breakfast from $40/68; ❋@) It's great to find a home away from home, and this historic cottage close to town has four cosy rooms and a relaxed lounge and country kitchen. For added privacy there's a separate motel-style section up front with en suite rooms. Its ultra-relaxed owner, Mark, is knowledgeable about the area.

Port Bayou   B&B $$
(☑03-5598 6009; www.portbayou.portcampbell. nu; 52 Lord St; d cottage from $185; ❋) Choose from the cosy in-house B&B or a rustic self-contained cottage fitted with exposed ceiling beams and corrugated-tin walls (we'd go for the cottage).

Eating & Drinking

12 Rocks Cafe Bar   CAFE $$
(19 Lord St; mains $21-37; ⊙9.30am-11pm) Watch flotsam wash up on the beach from this busy eatery, which has perfect beachfront views. Try a local Otways beer with a pasta or seafood main, or just duck in for a coffee.

Port Campbell Hotel   PUB
(40 Lord St; ⊙11am-1am Mon-Sat, noon-11pm Sun) Head in for a beer and a feed with the locals. Kitchen closes at 8.30pm.

ℹ Information

Port Campbell Visitor Centre (☑1300 137 255; www.visit12apostles.com.au; 26 Morris St; ⊙9am-5pm) Stacks of regional and accommodation information and interesting shipwreck displays – the anchor from the *Loch Ard* is out the front. Offers free use of binoculars and GPS equipment.

Warrnambool

POP 29,284

Warrnambool was originally a whaling and sealing station – now it's booming as a major regional commercial and whale-watching centre. Its historic buildings, waterways and tree-lined streets are attractive, and there's a large population of students.

◉ Sights & Activities

Sheltered Lady Bay, with fortifications at the breakwater at its western end, is the main swimming beach. Logan's Beach has the best surf and there are breaks at Levy's Beach and Second Bay.

★**Flagstaff Hill
Maritime Village**   HISTORIC SITE
See p25.

**Rundell's Mahogany
Trail Rides**   HORSE RIDING
(☑0408 589 546; www.rundellshorseriding.com.au; 1½hr beach ride $65) Get to know some of Warrnambool's quiet beach spots on horseback.

🛏 Sleeping

**Warrnambool Beach
Backpackers**   HOSTEL $
(☑03-5562 4874; www.beachbackpackers.com.au; 17 Stanley St; dm/d from $26/80; @ 🕏) A short stroll to the beach, this hostel has all backpackers' needs covered, with huge living area, kitchsy Aussie-themed bar, internet access, kitchen and free pick-up service. Its rooms are clean and good value, and it hires out surfboards and bikes. Vanpackers pay $12 per person to stay here.

Hotel Warrnambool   PUB $$
(☑03-5562 2377; www.hotelwarrnambool.com.au; cnr Koroit & Kepler Sts; d incl breakfast without/with bathroom from $110/140; ✳ 🕏) Renovations to this historic 1894 hotel have seen rooms upgraded to the more boutique end of the scale, while still keeping its classic pub-accommodation feel.

Lighthouse Lodge   GUESTHOUSE $$
(www.lighthouselodge.com.au; Flagstaff Hill; d/house from $155/375; ✳ 🕏) Once the former harbour master's residence, this charming weatherboard cottage can be rented as the entire house or separate rooms. It has a grassy area overlooking the Maritime Village and coastline. In the village there's also lodging in the Garrison Camp ($25 per person), a unique option for budget travellers

Great Ocean Road, near Lorne

WHALES AT WARRNAMBOOL

In the 19th century Warrnambool's whale industry involved hunting them with harpoons, but these days they're a major tourist attraction, with crowds gathering to see them frolic offshore on their migration between May and September. Southern right whales are the most common visitors, heading from Antarctica to these more temperate waters.

While whales can be seen all along the coastline. the best place to see them is at Warrnambool's Logan's Beach whale-watching platform. Sightings aren't guaranteed, but you've got a very good chance of spotting them breaching and slapping their tails about as they nurse their bubs in the waters. Call ahead to the visitor centre to check if whales are about, or see www.visitwarrnambool.com.au for latest sightings.

within small wooden A-frame bunk cabins. BYO linen.

Eating

★ Kermond's Hamburgers　　BURGERS $
(☑ 03-5562 4854; 151 Lava St; burgers $8; ⊙ 9am-9.30pm) Likely not much has changed at this burger joint since it opened in 1949, with Laminex tables, wood-panelled walls and classic milkshakes served in stainless-steel tumblers. Its burgers are an institution.

Bojangles　　PIZZA $$
(☑ 03-5562 8751; www.bojanglespizza.com.au; 61 Liebig St; mains $16-31; ⊙ 5-10pm; ☑) A step above your usual country pizza places, with seriously delicious thin-crust pizzas.

Hotel Warrnambool　　PUB FOOD $$
(www.hotelwarrnambool.com.au; cnr Koroit & Kepler Sts; lunch mains $12-27, dinner mains $28-34; ⊙ noon-late; ☑) One of Victoria's best coastal pubs, Hotel Warrnambool mixes pub charm with bohemian character and serves wood-fired pizzas, among other gastro-pub fare.

Information

Warrnambool Visitor Centre (☑ 1800 637 725; www.visitwarrnambool.com.au; Merri St; ⊙ 9am-5pm) For the latest on whale sightings, plus bike maps and several walking maps. Also has bicycle hire ($30 per day).

Getting There & Away

Warrnambool is an hour's drive west of Port Campbell on the B100.

Port Fairy

POP 2835

Port Fairy is a charming town with a relaxed vibe, heritage buildings, colourful fishing boats and wide, tree-lined streets; many of which date back to the 19th century when

the town was settled as a base for whaling and sealing.

Sights & Activities

Battery Hill　　HISTORIC SITE
Located across the bridge from the picturesque harbour, Battery Hill is worthy of exploration, with cannons and fortifications positioned here in 1887 to protect the town from foreign warships. You'll also encounter resident black wallabies. It was originally used as a flagstaff, so the views are good.

Self-Guided Walking Tours　　WALKING TOUR
Pick up a range of maps and brochures at the visitor centre that will guide you through various aspects of the town's heritage. It also has maps for the popular Maritime & Shipwreck Heritage Walk, while architecture buffs will want to buy a copy of *Historic Buildings of Port Fairy*.

Go Surf　　SURFING
(☑ 0408 310 001; www.gosurf.com.au; 2hr lesson $40, board hire 2hr/1 day $25/50) Surf school and stand-up paddle board tours.

Festivals & Events

★ Port Fairy Folk Festival　　MUSIC
See p21.

Sleeping

Much of Port Fairy's holiday accommodation is managed by agents. The visitor centre (p88) offers a free booking service. The Port Fairy Accommodation Centre (☑ 03-5568 3150; www.portfairyaccom.com.au; 2/54 Sackville St) is a local accommodation booking service, while Port Fairy Holiday Rentals (☑ 03-5568 1066; www.lockettrealestate.com.au; 62 Sackville St) operates as a local clearing house for accommodation.

THE SHIPWRECK COAST

In the era of sailing ships, Victoria's beautiful and rugged southwest coastline was one of the most treacherous on Earth. Between the 1830s and 1930s, more than 200 ships were torn asunder along the so-called Shipwreck Coast between Cape Otway and Port Fairy. From the early 1850s to late 1880s, Victoria's gold rush and subsequent economic boom brought countless shiploads of prospectors and hopefuls from Europe, North America and China. After spending months at sea, many vessels (and lives) were lost on the 'home straight'.

The **lighthouses** along this coast – at Aireys Inlet, Cape Otway, Port Fairy and Warrnambool – are still operating and you'll find shipwreck museums, memorial plaques and anchors that tell the story of wrecks along this coast. The most famous is that of the iron-hulled clipper **Loch Ard**, which foundered off Mutton Bird Island. Of the 56 people on board, only two survived by being washed into a gorge – since renamed **Loch Ard Gorge** (p24).

Port Fairy YHA
HOSTEL **$**

(☑ 03-5568 2468; www.portfairyhostel.com.au; 8 Cox St; dm $26-30, s/tw/d from $41.50/70/75; @ 🛜) In the rambling 1844 home of merchant William Rutledge, this friendly, well-run hostel has a large kitchen, a pool table, free cable TV and peaceful gardens.

★ Douglas on River
B&B **$$**

(www.douglasonriver.com.au; 85 Gipps St; r incl breakfast from $160; 🛜) On the waterfront along the wharf, this 1852 heritage guesthouse lays claims to being the oldest in Port Fairy and is a great choice for those seeking boutique accommodation. The lovely front lawn and common area are both perfect for relaxing, and it does wonderful breakfasts using local produce.

Pelican Waters
CABIN **$$**

(☑ 03-5568 1002; www.pelicanwatersportfairy.com. au; 34 Regent St; cabins from $100; ❄) Why stay in a hotel when you can sleep in a train? This beautifully presented farm property has cabins as well as rooms in converted old-school Melbourne suburban MET trains. Has alpacas and llamas, too.

✖ Eating & Drinking

Pantry Door at Basalt
CAFE **$$**

(☑ 03-5568 7442; 1131 Princes Hwy, Killarney; mains $12-26; ⊙ 7.30am-noon Mon, to 4.30pm Wed-Sun; 🛜) Just outside Port Fairy, in the township of Killarney, this bluestone homestead cafe focuses on seasonal local produce and has an outdoor deck among fruit trees. Next door is **Basalt Wines** (see p25).

Stump Hotel
PUB **$$**

(☑ 03-5568 1044; www.caledonianinnportfairy. com.au; 41 Bank St; mains $16-22; ⊙ noon-late) Victoria's oldest continuously licensed pub (1844), the Stump, aka Caledonian Inn, has a beer garden and pub grub. Also has no-frills motel rooms from $100.

★ Merrijig Kitchen
MODERN AUSTRALIAN **$$$**

(☑ 03-5568 2324; www.merrijiginn.com; 1 Campbell St; mains $28-38; ⊙ 6-9pm Thu-Mon; 🛜) One of coastal Victoria's most atmospheric restaurants; warm yourself by the open fire and enjoy superb dining with a menu that changes according to what's seasonal. Delectable food with great service.

① Information

Port Fairy Visitor Centre (☑ 03-5568 2682; www.visitportfairy-moyneshire.com.au; Bank St; ⊙ 9am-5pm) Provides spot-on tourist information, walking tour brochures, V/Line tickets and bike hire (half/full day $15/25).

Loch Ard Gorge (p24)
RAIMUND LINKE/GETTY IMAGES ©

GREAT OCEAN ROAD DISTANCES & TIMES

ROUTE	DISTANCE	TIME
Melbourne–Geelong	75km	1hr
Geelong–Torquay	21km	15-20min
Torquay–Anglesea	16km	15min
Anglesea–Aireys Inlet	10km	10min
Aireys Inlet–Lorne	19km	20min
Lorne–Apollo Bay	45km	1hr
Apollo Bay–Port Campbell	96km	1½hr
Port Campbell–Warrnambool	66km	1hr
Warrnambool–Port Fairy	28km	20min
Port Fairy–Portland	72km	1hr
Portland–Melbourne	via Great Ocean Road 440km/via Hamilton Hwy 358km	6½hr/4¼hr

ⓘ Getting There & Away

Port Fairy is 20 minutes' drive west of Warrnambool on the A1.

Portland

POP 9950

Portland's claim to fame is as Victoria's first European settlement, founded as a whaling and sealing base in the early 1800s. Despite its colonial history and architecture and its size, blue-collared Portland lacks a real drawcard, which sees it fall short of its potential. There are some good beaches and surf breaks outside town.

◉ Sights & Activities

Whales often visit during winter; see www.whalemail.com.au for latest sightings.

Historic Waterfront　　　　WATERFRONT
(Cliff St) The grassy precinct overlooking the harbour has several heritage bluestone buildings. The **History House** (☑03-5522 2266; Cliff St; adult/child $3/2; ☉10am-noon & 1-4pm), located in the former town hall (1863), has an interesting museum detailing Portland's colonial past. **Customs House** (1850) has a fascinating display of confiscated booty, including a stuffed black bear. Also here is the 1845 **courthouse**, the 1886 **Rocket Shed**, with a display of ship rescue equipment, and the 1889 **battery**, built as defence against feared Russian invasion.

Self-guided Walking Tours　　WALKING TOUR
The tourist office offers several self-guided walking-tour brochures, including a **heritage building** tour and one that traces the steps of **St Mary MacKillop's** time in Portland.

⌷ Sleeping

Annesley House　　　　BOUTIQUE HOTEL $$
(☑0429 852 235; www.annesleyhouse.com.au; 60 Julia St; d from $150; ❋🐾) This recently restored former doctor's mansion (c 1878) has six very different self-contained rooms, some featuring claw-foot baths and lovely views. All have a unique sense of style.

Clifftop Accommodation　　GUESTHOUSE $$
(☑03-5523 1126; www.portlandaccommodation.com.au; 13 Clifton Ct; d from $140; ❋🐾) The panoramic ocean views from the balconies here are incredible. Three self-contained rooms are huge, with big brass beds, telescopes and a modern maritime feel.

✕ Eating

Deegan Seafoods　　　　FISH & CHIPS $
(106 Percy St; mains from $10; ☉9am-6pm Mon-Fri) This fish-and-chip shop famously serves up the freshest fish in Victoria.

Cafe Bahloo　　　　　　CAFE $$
(85 Cliff St; mains $12-29; ☉7.30am-3.30pm Tue-Sat) Housed in the original bluestone watchkeeper's house across from the harbour, Bahloo serves good breakfasts and coffee.

ⓘ Information

Portland Visitor Centre (☑1800 035 567; www.visitportland.com.au; Lee Breakwater Rd; ☉9am-5pm) In a modern building on the waterfront, this excellent information centre has a stack of suggestions of things to do and see.

ⓘ Getting There & Away

Portland is a one-hour drive west of Port Fairy on the A1.

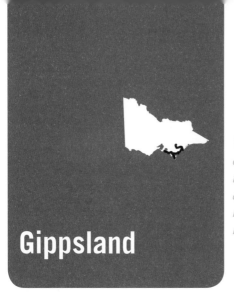

With only a handful of what could be considered large towns, even fewer people and an abundance of wildlife and natural stghts Gippsland is a rural treat.

Gippsland

Phillip Island

POP 9406

Famous for the Penguin Parade and Motorcycle Grand Prix racing circuit, Phillip Island attracts a curious mix of surfers, petrolheads and international tourists making a beeline for those little penguins.

At its heart Phillip Island is still a farming community, but nature has conspired to turn it into one of Victoria's hottest tourist destinations. Apart from the nightly waddling of the penguins, there's a large seal colony, abundant bird life around the Rhyll wetlands and a koala colony. The rugged south coast has some fabulous surf beaches and the swell of tourists – the holiday population jumps to around 40,000 over summer – means there's a swag of family attractions, plenty of accommodation and a buzzing, if unexciting, cafe and restaurant scene in the island capital, Cowes. Visit in winter, though, and you'll find a very quiet place where the local population of farmers, surfers and hippies goes about its business.

◉ Sights & Activities

Cowes Main Beach is calm and safe for swimming – head over to the long Cowes East Beach for a quieter time. The best surf beaches are along the southern coast. Spectacular Cape Woolamai is the most popular surf beach, but rips and currents make it suitable only for experienced surf-

ers. Beginners and families head to Smiths Beach, which is often teeming with surf-school groups. Both are patrolled in summer. Berrys Beach is another beautiful spot and usually quieter than Woolamai or Smiths. Around the Nobbies, Cat Bay and Flynns Reef will often be calm when the wind is blowing onshore at the Woolamai and Smiths areas.

★ Penguin Parade   WILDLIFE RESERVE
(☑ 03-5951 2800; www.penguins.org.au; Summerland Beach; adult/child/family $23.80/11.90/59.50; ☉ 10am-dusk, penguins arrive at sunset) The Penguin Parade attracts more than 500,000 visitors annually to see the little penguins (*Eudyptula minor),* the world's smallest penguins, and probably the cutest of their kind. The penguin complex includes concrete amphitheatres that hold up to 3800 spectators who come to see the little fellas just after sunset as they waddle from the sea to their burrows.

Penguin numbers swell in summer, after breeding, but they're in residence year-round. After the parade, hang around the boardwalks for a closer view as the stragglers search for their burrows and mates. Bring warm clothing. There are a variety of specialised tours (www.penguins.org.au; adult $44-80), where you can be accompanied by rangers to explain the behaviour of penguins, or see the penguins from the vantage of a Skybox (an elevated platform). There's also a cafe and an interpretive centre at the complex.

Phillip Island

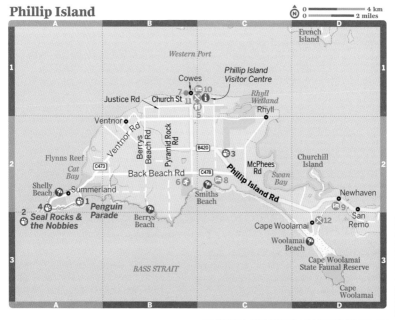

Koala Conservation Centre   ZOO
(☑03-5951 2800; www.penguins.org.au; 1810 Phillip Island Rd, Cowes; adult/child/family $11.90/5.95/29.75; ☉10am-5pm, extended hours in summer) From the boardwalks here you're certain to see koalas chewing on eucalyptus leaves or dozing away – they sleep about 20 hours a day!

★**Seal Rocks &
the Nobbies**   WILDLIFE WATCHING
(☉11am-5pm) The Nobbies are a couple of large, craggy, offshore rocks at the island's southwestern tip. Beyond them are Seal Rocks, which are inhabited by Australia's largest fur-seal colony. The **Nobbies Centre** (☑03-5951 2852; www.penguins.org.au; ☉11am-1hr before sunset) FREE offers great views over the Nobbies and the 6000-or-so distant Australian fur seals that sun themselves there. You can view the seals from boardwalk binoculars or use the centre's underwater cameras ($5). The centre also has some fascinating interactive exhibits, a kids' games room and a cafe.

★**Phillip Island
Grand Prix Circuit**   ADVENTURE SPORTS
(☑03-5952 9400; Back Beach Rd) Even when the motorbikes aren't racing, petrolheads love the Grand Prix Motor Racing Circuit, which was souped up for the Australian Motorcycle

Phillip Island

◎ Top Sights
1 Penguin Parade.....................................A2
2 Seal Rocks & the Nobbies A3

◎ Sights
3 Koala Conservation Centre C2
4 Nobbies Centre.....................................A2

◎ Activities, Courses & Tours
5 Island Surfboards C1
6 Phillip Island Grand Prix Circuit B2
7 Wildlife Coast Cruises B1

◎ Sleeping
8 Clifftop..C2
9 Island Accommodation YHA...............D2
10 Waves Apartments C1

◎ Eating
11 Fig & Olive at Cowes B1
12 White Salt..D3

Grand Prix in 1989. The visitor centre runs **guided circuit tours** (www.phillipislandcircuit. com.au; adult/child/family $22/13/57; ☉tours 2pm), or check out the **History of Motorsport Museum** (adult/child/family $15/8/38). The more adventurous can cut laps of the track with a racing driver in hotted-up V8s ($330; bookings essential).

BUNURONG MARINE & COASTAL PARK

This marine and coastal park offers some of Australia's best snorkelling and diving, and a stunning, cliff-hugging drive between Inverloch and Cape Paterson. It is also the location of dinosaur remains dating back 120 million years. Eagles Nest, Shack Bay, the Caves and Twin Reefs are great for **snorkelling**, the Oaks is the locals' favourite **surf beach**, while the Caves is where the **dinosaur dig** action is at.

SEAL Diving Services (☑ 03-5174 3434; www.sealdivingservices.com.au; 7/27 Princes Hwy, Traralgon) SEAL offers PADI open-water dive courses in Inverloch in summer. Also available are one-day dives for beginners and experienced divers, kids' programs and weekend trips for certified divers at Bunurong Marine and Coastal Park.

Drive yourself in a go-kart around a scale replica of the track with **Phillip Island Circuit Go Karts** (per 10/20/30min $35/60/80).

Island Surfboards   SURFING
(☑ 03-5952 3443; www.islandsurfboards.com.au; 65 Smiths Beach Rd, Smiths Beach; lessons $65, surfboard hire per hr/day $12.50/40) Island Surfboards can start your waxhead career with wetsuit hire and lessons for all standards. Also has a store at **Cowes** (☑ 03-5952 2578; www.islandsurfboards.com.au; 147 Thompson Ave; board hire per hour/day $12.50/40).

Tours

Go West   TOUR
(☑ 1300 736 551, 03-9485 5290; www.gowest.com.au; tour $135) One-day tour from Melbourne that includes lunch and iPod commentary in several languages. Includes entry to the Penguin Parade.

Wildlife Coast Cruises   BOAT TOUR
(☑ 03-5952 3501; www.wildlifecoastcruises.com.au; Rotunda Bldg, Cowes Jetty; seal watching adult/child $72/49; ⊙ 2pm Fri-Wed May-Sep, 2pm & 4.30pm daily Oct-Apr) Runs a variety of cruises, including seal-watching, twilight and cape cruises. Also runs a two-hour cruise to French Island (adult/child $30/20) and a full-day cruise to Wilsons Promontory ($190/140).

Festivals & Events

Australian Motorcycle Grand Prix   SPORTS
(www.motogp.com.au) The island's biggest event – three days of bike action in October.

Sleeping & Eating

Island Accommodation YHA   HOSTEL $
(☑ 03-5956 6123; www.theislandaccommodation.com.au; 10-12 Phillip Island Rd, Newhaven; dm/d from $35/165; @ 🛜) 𝄖 This large, purpose-built backpackers has huge identical living areas on each floor, complete with table-tennis tables and cosy fireplaces for winter. Its rooftop deck has terrific views and its eco-credentials are excellent. Cheapest dorms sleep 12 and doubles are motel standard.

Waves Apartments   APARTMENT $$
(☑ 03-5952 1351; www.thewaves.com.au; 1 Esplanade, Cowes; d from $195; ❄🛜) These slick apartments overlook Cowes Main Beach, so you can't beat the balcony views if you go for a beachfront unit. The modern, self-contained apartments come with spa, and balcony or patio.

Clifftop   BOUTIQUE HOTEL $$$
(☑ 03-5952 1033; www.clifftop.com.au; 1 Marlin St, Smiths Beach; d $235-300; ❄) It's hard to imagine a better location for your island stay than perched above Smiths Beach. Of the seven luxurious suites here, the top four have ocean views and private balconies, while the downstairs rooms open onto gardens – all have fluffy beds and slick decor.

White Salt   FISH & CHIPS $
(☑ 03-5956 6336; 7 Vista Pl, Cape Woolamai; fish from $6.50, meal packs from $15; ⊙ 5-8pm Wed, Thu & Sun, noon-8.30pm Fri & Sat) White Salt serves the best fish and chips on the island – select from fish fillets and hand-cut chips, tempura prawns and marinated barbecue octopus salad with corn, pesto and lemon.

Fig & Olive at Cowes   MODERN AUSTRALIAN $$
(☑ 03-5952 2655; www.figandoliveatcowes.com.au; 115 Thompson Ave, Cowes; mains $24-38; ⊙ 9am-late Wed-Mon) A groovy mix of timber, stone and lime-green decor makes this a relaxing place to enjoy a beautifully presented meal, or a late-night cocktail. The eclectic menu is strong on seafood and moves from paella or pork belly to wood-fired Tasmanian salmon.

ℹ️ Information

Phillip Island Visitor Centre (☎1300 366 422; www.visitphillipisland.com; 895 Phillip Island Tourist Rd, Newhaven; ⏰9am-5pm, to 6pm school holidays) The main visitor centre for the island is on the main road at Newhaven, and there's a smaller centre at Cowes (cnr Thompson & Church Sts, Cowes). Both sell the Three Parks Pass (adult/child/family $36/18/90), covering the Penguin Parade, Koala Conservation Centre and Churchill Island Heritage Farm, and the main centre has a free accommodation- and tour-booking service.

ℹ️ Getting There & Away

About 140km from Melbourne, Phillip Island can only be accessed by car across the bridge between San Remo and Newhaven. From Melbourne take the Monash Fwy and exit at Pakenham, joining the South Gippsland Hwy at Koo Wee Rup.

Koonwarra

Tucked away in rolling dairy country along the South Gippsland Hwy, this tiny township has built itself a reputation as something of a niche foodie destination, thanks to its cooking school and general store.

◉ Sights & Activities

Farmers Market   MARKET
See p29.

Milly & Romeo's Artisan Bakery & Cooking School   COURSE
See p29.

🛏️ Sleeping & Eating

Lyre Bird Hill Winery & Guest House   B&B **$$**
(☎03-5664 3204; www.lyrebirdhill.com.au; 370 Inverloch Rd; s/d $125/175; ⏰cellar door 10am-5pm Wed-Mon Oct, Nov & Feb-Apr, daily Dec & Jan, by appointment May-Sep; ❄) Stay among the vines 4km southwest of Koonwarra. The quaint, old-fashioned B&B has light-filled rooms overlooking the garden, while the self-contained country-style cottage is perfect for a family. The vineyard is right next door.

Koonwarra Food & Wine Store   MODERN AUSTRALIAN **$$**
See p29.

ℹ️ Getting There & Away

Koonwarra is served by buses running between Korumburra and Foster three times a day weekdays and up to six times daily on weekends. By road the town is 32km southwest of Korumburra and 21km northeast of Inverloch.

Korumburra

POP 3350

The first sizeable town along the South Gippsland Hwy if you're coming from Melbourne, Korumburra is scenically situated on

D. PARER & E. PARER-COOK/MINDEN PICTURES/GETTY IMAGES ©

Little penguins, Phillip Island (p90)

Wilsons Promontory National Park

the edge of the Strzelecki Ranges. It makes a decent pause on your way to Wilsons Prom.

⊙ Sights

Coal Creek Village   MUSEUM
(☑ 03-5655 1811; www.coalcreekvillage.com.au; 12 Silkstone Rd; ☉ 10am-4.30pm Thu-Mon, daily during school holidays) **FREE** Coal Creek Village is a re-creation of a 19th-century mining town. It's a little less polished and touristy than other similar places in Victoria, which may appeal to many.

❶ Getting There & Away

V/Line (☑ 1800 800 007; www.vline.com.au) V/Line coaches from Melbourne's Southern Cross Station run to Korumburra ($12.80, 1¾ hours) up to seven times daily.

Wilsons Promontory National Park

If you like wilderness bushwalking, stunning coastal scenery and secluded white-sand beaches, you'll absolutely love this place. The Prom, as it's affectionately known, is one of the most popular national parks in Australia. Hardly surprising, given its accessibility from Melbourne, its network of more than 80km of walking tracks, its swimming and surf beaches and the abundant wildlife. The southernmost part of mainland Australia, the Prom once

formed part of a land bridge that allowed people to walk to Tasmania.

Tidal River, 30km from the park entrance, is the hub, although there's no fuel to be had here. It's home to the Parks Victoria office, a general store, cafe and accommodation. The wildlife around Tidal River is incredibly tame.

🏃 Activities

There's an extensive choice of marked walking trails, taking you through forests, marshes, valleys of tree ferns, low granite mountains and along beaches lined with sand dunes. The Parks Victoria office at Tidal River has brochures with details of walks, from 15-minute strolls to multiday hikes. Even non-walkers can enjoy some of the park's beauty, with car-park access off the Tidal River road leading to beaches and lookouts.

Swimming is safe at the gorgeous beaches at Norman Bay (Tidal River) and around the headland at Squeaky Beach – the ultra-fine quartz sand here really does squeak beneath your feet!

☞ Tours

Bunyip Tours   BUS TOUR
(☑ 1300 286 947; www.bunyiptours.com; tours from $120; ☉ Wed & Sun, plus Fri in summer) 🌱 Proudly carbon-neutral, Bunyip Tours offers a one-day guided tour to the Prom from

Wilsons Promontory National Park

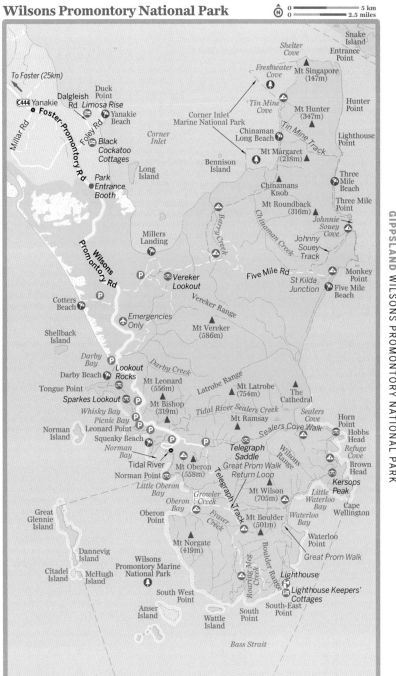

0 — 5 km
0 — 2.5 miles

Snake Island
Entrance Point
Shelter Cove
Mt Singapore (147m)
Freshwater Cove
Tin Mine Cove
Mt Hunter (347m)
Hunter Point
Corner Inlet Marine National Park
Chinaman Long Beach
Tin Mine Track
Lighthouse Point
To Foster (25km)
Duck Point
Dalgleish Rd
Limosa Rise
C444 Yanakie
Foster-Promontory Rd
Foley Rd
Yanakie Beach
Corner Inlet
Mt Margaret (218m)
Three Mile Beach
Black Cockatoo Cottages
Bennison Island
Chinamans Knob
Three Mile Point
Long Island
Mt Roundback (316m)
Millar Rd
Park Entrance Booth
Johnnie Souey Cove
Chinaman Creek
Johnny Souey Track
Millers Landing
Barry Creek
Wilsons Promontory Rd
Vereker Lookout
Five Mile Rd
St Kilda Junction
Monkey Point
Five Mile Beach
Cotters Beach
Emergencies Only
Vereker Range
Mt Vereker (586m)
Shellback Island
Darby Bay
Lookout Rocks
Darby Creek
Darby Beach
Mt Leonard (556m)
Latrobe Range
Mt Latrobe (754m)
The Cathedral
Tongue Point
Sparkes Lookout
Mt Bishop (319m)
Tidal River
Sealers Creek
Mt Ramsay
Sealers Cove
Horn Point
Whisky Bay
Picnic Bay
Leonard Point
Sealers Cove Walk
Hobbs Head
Norman Island
Squeaky Beach
Telegraph Saddle
Wilsons Range
Refuge Cove
Brown Head
Norman Bay
Tidal River
Great Prom Walk Return Loop
Kersops Peak
Norman Point
Mt Oberon (558m)
Little Oberon Bay
Oberon Bay
Growler Creek
Mt Wilson (705m)
Little Waterloo Bay
Cape Wellington
Great Glennie Island
Oberon Point
Fraser Creek
Mt Boulder (501m)
Waterloo Bay
Dannevig Island
Mt Norgate (419m)
Telegraph Track
Waterloo Point
Citadel Island
McHugh Island
Wilsons Promontory Marine National Park
Roaring Meg Creek
Boulder Range
Great Prom Walk
Lighthouse
South West Point
Lighthouse Keepers' Cottages
Anser Island
Wattle Island
South Point
South-East Point
Bass Strait

GIPPSLAND WILSONS PROMONTORY NATIONAL PARK

95

Melbourne, with the option of staying on another two days to explore by yourself.

First Track Adventures ADVENTURE TOUR
(☎ 03-5634 2761; www.firsttrack.com.au) This Yarragon-based company organises customised bushwalking, canoeing and abseiling trips to the Prom for individuals and groups. Prices vary according to group size and activity.

🛏 Sleeping

★**Lighthouse Keepers'**
Cottages COTTAGE $$$
(☑ Parks Victoria 13 19 63; www.parkweb.vic.gov.au; d cottage $334-371, 12-bed cottage per person from $133.80) These isolated, heritage-listed 1850s cottages with thick granite walls, attached to a working lightstation on a pimple of land that juts out into the wild ocean, are a real getaway. Kick back after the 19km hike from Tidal River and watch ships or whales passing by. The cottages have shared facilities, including a fully equipped kitchen.

🛏 Tidal River

★**Wilderness Retreat** SAFARI TENT $$$
(www.wildernessretreats.com.au; d $312, extra person $25) Nestled in bushland at Tidal River, these luxury safari tents, each with their own deck, bathroom, queen-sized beds, heating and a communal tent kitchen, sleep up to four people and are pretty cool. It's like being on an African safari with a kookaburra soundtrack.

🛏 Yanakie & Foster

The tiny settlement of Yanakie offers the closest accommodation – from cabins and camping to luxury cottages – outside the park boundaries. Foster, the nearest main town, has a backpackers and several motels.

Prom Coast Backpackers HOSTEL $
(☑ 0427 875 735; www.promcoastyha.com.au; 40 Station Rd, Foster; dm/d from $35/70; @) The closest backpacker hostel to the park is this friendly YHA in Foster. The cosy renovated cottage sleeps only 10, so it's always intimate.

Black Cockatoo Cottages COTTAGE $$
(☑ 03-5687 1306; www.blackcockatoo.com; 60 Foley Rd, Yanakie; d $140-170, 6-person house $250) You can take in glorious views of the national park without leaving your very comfortable bed – or breaking the bank – in these private, stylish, black-timber cottages. There are three modern cottages and a three-bedroom house.

TOP PROM WALKS

From Christmas to the end of January a free shuttle bus operates between the Tidal River visitor car park and the Telegraph Saddle car park (a nice way to start the Great Prom Walk).

Great Prom Walk The most popular long-distance hike is a moderate 45km circuit across to Sealers Cove from Tidal River, down to Refuge Cove, Waterloo Bay and the lighthouse, returning to Tidal River via Oberon Bay. Allow three days and coordinate your walk with tide times, as creek crossings can be hazardous. It's possible to visit or stay at the lighthouse by prior arrangement with the Parks office.

Sealers Cove Walk The best overnight hike, this two-day walk starts at Telegraph Saddle and heads down Telegraph Track to stay overnight at beautiful Little Waterloo Bay (12km, 4½ hours). The next day, walk on to Sealers Cove via Refuge Cove and return to Telegraph Saddle (24km, 7½ hours).

Lilly Pilly Gully Nature Walk An easy 5km (two-hour) walk through heathland and eucalypt forests, with lots of wildlife.

Mt Oberon Summit Starting from the Mt Oberon car park, this moderate-to-hard 7km (2½-hour) walk is an ideal introduction to the Prom with panoramic views from the summit. The free Mt Oberon shuttle bus can take you to the Telegraph Saddle car park and back.

Little Oberon Bay An easy-to-moderate 8km (three-hour) walk over sand dunes covered in coastal tea trees with beautiful views over Little Oberon Bay.

Squeaky Beach Nature Walk Another easy 5km return stroll through coastal tea tree and banksias to a sensational white-sand beach.

ℹ PROM ACCOMMODATION

Nothing beats a night at the Prom. The main accommodation base is Tidal River, but there are 11 bush-camping (outstation) areas around the Prom, all with pit or compost toilets, but no other facilities; you need to carry in your own drinking water.

Unpowered/powered **camp sites** with a vehicle and up to eight people start at $54.90/$61.10 per site. There are also wooden **huts** with bunks and kitchenettes but no bathrooms (4/6-bed hut from $98.50/150), and spacious and private self-contained **cabins** sleeping up to six people ($229.60 to $313.80).

Tidal River has 484 camp sites, but only 20 powered sites. For the Christmas school holiday period there's a ballot for sites (apply online by 30 June through Parks Victoria).

Parks Victoria (☑03-5680 9555, 13 19 63; www.parkweb.vic.gov.au; ⊘8.30am-4.30pm) The helpful visitor centre at Tidal River books all park accommodation, including permits for camping away from Tidal River.

Wilsons Prom & Surrounds Accommodation Service (www.promcountry.com.au) For bookings in the Prom's hinterland, use this service.

★ **Limosa Rise**　　　　COTTAGE $$$
(☑03-5687 1135; www.limosarise.com.au; 40 Dalgleish Rd, Yanakie; d $260-455; ❄) The views are stupendous from these luxury, self-contained cottages near the Prom entrance. The three tastefully appointed cottages (a studio, one bedroom and two bedroom) are fitted with full-length glass windows taking complete advantage of sweeping views across Corner Inlet and the Prom's mountains.

✗ Eating

**Tidal River General
Store & Cafe**　　　　CAFE $
(mains $5-24; ⊘9am-5pm Sun-Fri, to 6pm Sat) The Tidal River general store stocks grocery items and some camping equipment, but if you're hiking or staying a while it's cheaper to stock up in Foster. The attached cafe serves takeaway food such as pies and sandwiches, as well as breakfasts, light lunches and bistro-style meals on weekends and holidays.

ℹ Getting There & Away

Tidal River lies approximately 224km southeast of Melbourne. There's no direct public transport between Melbourne and the Prom.

Walhalla
POP 15

Just 35km north of the main road is Victoria's best-preserved and most charming historic town. Walhalla is secreted high in the green hills and forests of west Gippsland, and is made up of pretty period cottages and other timber buildings. Its setting is glorious; strung out along a deep, forested valley with Stringers Creek running through the centre of the township.

Gold was discovered here on 26 December 1862, although the first find was not registered until January 1863, which is when the gold rush really began. In its heyday, Walhalla's population stood at 5000, but fell to just 10 people by the end of the 20th century.

◉ Sights & Activities

The best way to see the town is on foot – take the **tramline walk** (45 minutes), which begins from opposite the general store soon after you enter town. Other good (and well-signposted) walks lead to the valley floor. Among them, a trail leads to the **Walhalla Cricket Ground** (2km, 45 minutes return). Another trail climbs to the extraordinary **Walhalla Cemetery** (20 minutes return), where the gravestones cling to the steep valley wall. Their inscriptions tell a sombre, yet fascinating, story of the town's history.

**Walhalla Historical
Museum**　　　　MUSEUM
(☑03-5165 6250; admission $2; ⊘10am-4pm) Located in the old post office in the group of restored shops along the main street, Walhalla Historical Museum also acts as an information centre and books the popular two-hour **ghost tours** (www.walhallaghosttour.info; adult/child/family $25/20/75; ⊘7.30pm Sat, 8.30pm Sat during daylight saving) on Saturday nights.

**Long Tunnel Extended
Gold Mine**　　　　MINE
(☑03-5165 6259; off Walhalla-Beardmore Rd; adult/child/family $19.50/13.50/49.50; ⊘1.30pm

WORTH A TRIP

BAW BAW NATIONAL PARK

Baw Baw National Park, an offshoot of the Great Dividing Range, is the southernmost region of Victoria's High Country. The Baw Baw Plateau and the forested valleys of the Thomson and Aberfeldy Rivers are wonderful places for bushwalking, with marked tracks through subalpine vegetation, ranging from open eucalypt stands to wet gullies and tall forests on the plateau. The highest points are Mt St Phillack (1566m) and Mt Baw Baw (1564m). The higher sections of the park are snow-covered in winter, when everyone heads for Baw Baw Village ski resort and the Mt St Gwinear cross-country skiing area. Quiet back roads (and the Australian Alps Walking Track) connect this region with Walhalla.

Mt Baw Baw Alpine Resort Management Board (☑03-5165 1136; www.mount-bawbaw.com.au; ⊗8.30am-7.30pm Sat-Thu, to 9.30pm Fri ski season, 9am-5pm rest of year) In the centre of the village, this office provides general tourist information and an accommodation service.

daily, plus noon & 3pm Sat, Sun & holidays) Relive the mining past with guided tours exploring Cohens Reef, once one of Australia's top reef-gold producers. Almost 14 tonnes of gold came out of this mine.

Walhalla Goldfields Railway   TRAIN
(☑03-5165 6280; www.walhallarail.com; adult/child/family return $20/15/50; ⊗from Walhalla Station 11am, 1pm & 3pm, from Thomson Station 11.40am, 1.40pm & 3.40pm Wed, Sat, Sun & public holidays) A star attraction is the scenic Walhalla Goldfields Railway, which offers a 20-minute ride between Walhalla and Thomson Stations (on the main road, 3.5km before Walhalla). The train snakes along Stringers Creek Gorge, passing lovely, forested gorge country and crossing a number of trestle bridges. There are daily departures in summer.

🛏 Sleeping & Eating

You can camp for free at **North Gardens**, a camp site with toilets and barbecues (but no showers) at the north end of the village.

Chinese Garden   CAMPGROUND **$**
(www.walhallaboard.org.au; off Main St; per person $25) At the northern end of town, this recently opened camping ground has full toilet and shower facilities, a laundrette and a barbecue area.

★**Walhalla Star Hotel**   HISTORIC HOTEL **$$**
(☑03-5165 6262; www.starhotel.com.au; Main St; d incl breakfast $189-249; ❄@🛜) The rebuilt historic Star offers stylish boutique accommodation with king-sized beds and simple but sophisticated designer decor, making good use of local materials such as corrugated-iron water tanks. Guests can dine at the in-house restaurant; others need to reserve in advance. Or you can get good breakfasts, pies, coffee and cake at the attached **Greyhorse Café** (mains from $5; ⊗10am-2pm).

Windsor House   B&B **$$**
(☑03-5165 6237; www.windsorhouse.com.au; off Walhalla Rd; d $170, ste $175-215) The five rooms and suites in this beautifully restored two-storey 1878 home are fittingly old fashioned and ghost free. No children under 12.

Walhalla Lodge Hotel   PUB FOOD **$$**
(☑03-5165 6226; Main St; mains $15-28; ⊗noon-2pm & 6-9pm Wed-Mon) The Wally Pub is a cosy, one-room pub decked out with prints of old Walhalla and serving good-value counter meals – think burgers, pasta, schnitzels and T-bone steaks.

ⓘ Getting There & Away

Walhalla lies approximately 180km east of Melbourne. There's no public transport. By road, the town can be reached along a lovely, winding forest drive from Moe or Traralgon.

Mornington Peninsula

The boot-shaped peninsula making up the eastern side of Port Phillip Bay is home to world-class wineries, family-friendly beaches and an array of activities – all within a few hours' drive from Melbourne.

Mornington

POP 22,421

Pretty Mornington, with its cute bathing boxes and swimming beaches, is the gateway to the peninsula's holiday coastal strip – just beyond the reaches of Melbourne's urban sprawl. Originally part of the lands of the Boonwurrung people, it was founded as a European township in 1854. The town thrived and by 1890 there were steamers and a daily train service from Melbourne – now sadly defunct.

◎ Sights & Activities

For views over the harbour, take a walk along the 1850s pier and around the Schnapper Point foreshore boardwalk past the Matthew Flinders monument that commemorates his 1802 landing. Mothers Beach is the main swimming beach, while at Fossil Beach, where limestone was mined in the 1860s, there are remains of a lime-burning kiln. Fossils found here date back 25 million years! At Mills Beach you can see colourful and photogenic bathing boxes.

Historic Buildings   NOTABLE BUILDINGS
There are several grand old buildings around Main St, including the 1892 Grand Hotel. The Old Court House, on the corner of Main St and the Esplanade (C783), was built in 1860,

and the Police Lock-Up behind it was built in 1862. On the opposite corner is the Old Post Office Museum (☑03-5976 3203; cnr Main St & The Esplanade; admission by donation; ◎1.30-4.30pm Sun & public holidays, 11am-3pm Wed in summer) in the 1863 post office building. Nearby is a monument to the 15 members of Mornington's football team who lost their lives when their boat, *Process*, sank while returning from a game against Mordialloc in 1892.

Mornington Botanical
Rose Gardens   GARDENS
(cnr Mornington-Tyabb Rd & Dunns Rd) FREE Away from the beach, the Mornington Botanical Rose Gardens is a beautifully landscaped garden with over 4000 flowers.

Mornington Peninsula
Regional Gallery   GALLERY
(☑03-5975 4395; www.mprg.mornpen.vic.gov. au; Dunns Rd; adult/child $4/free; ◎10am-5pm Tue-Sun) In the Civic Reserve alongside the Botanical Rose Gardens, the outstanding Mornington Peninsula Regional Gallery has changing exhibitions and a permanent collection of Australian prints and paintings.

Mornington Street
Market   MARKET
(Main St; ◎9am-3pm Wed) Every Wednesday, the Mornington Street Market takes over Main St with stalls and crafts.

Mornington Railway
HISTORIC RAILWAY

(☑1300 767 274; www.morningtonrailway.org.au; Mornington train station; return adult/child $16/5) On the first three Sundays of each month popular Mornington Railway runs steam locomotives between Mornington and Moorooduc.

Schnapper Point
Boat Hire
BOATING

(☑03-5975 5479; www.fishingmornington.com; Boatshed 7, Scout Beach) Rents out kayaks (first hour $30) and small motor boats (from $85 for two hours), and sells fishing tackle and bait.

🛏 Sleeping & Eating

Main St is lined with cafes and restaurants, particularly at the bay end.

Royal Hotel
HOTEL $$

(☑03-5975 9115; www.theroyal.com.au; 770 The Esplanade; d from $150; ❋) Classified by the National Trust, the Royal is tastefully renovated, offering authentic old-world accommodation in a range of rooms and bay views. The latest round of renovations was underway when we last visited but we expect the best rooms to still be the balcony suites with bathrooms and sea views.

The Rocks
SEAFOOD $$

(☑03-5973 5599; www.therocksmornington.com.au; 1 Schnapper Point Dr; mains $18-36; ☺8am-10pm) At the Mornington Yacht Club, this restaurant, with an open-sided deck overlooking the marina, is the perfect place for a drink or light meal. The restaurant is strong on fresh seafood, with oysters done every which way.

Afghan Marco Polo
MIDDLE EASTERN $$

(☑03-5975 5154; www.afghanmarcopolo.com.au; 9-11 Main St; mains $23-37; ☺6pm-late) Marco Polo is an atmospheric place with Persian rugs and brass hookahs that serves traditional Afghan cuisine. Kebabs, kormas, *boranis* and *kulfi* ice cream – a Central Asian mash up!

ⓘ Information

Mornington Library (☑03-5950 1820; Vancouver St; ☺9am-2pm Mon & Sat, to 8pm Tue & Thu, to 6pm Wed & Fri; ☎) Free internet access.

Mornington Visitors Centre (☑03-5975 1644; www.visitmorningtonpeninsula.org; 320 Main St; ☺9am-5pm) Has useful regional information and a Mornington walking-tour map.

Sorrento
POP 1448

Historic Sorrento is the standout town on the Mornington Peninsula for its beautiful limestone buildings, ocean and bay beaches, and buzzing seaside summer atmosphere. This was the site of Victoria's first official European settlement, established by an expedition of convicts, marines, civil officers and free settlers who arrived from England in 1803.

Sorrento boasts some of the best cafes and restaurants on the peninsula, and the main street is lined with galleries, boutiques, and craft and antique shops – naturally, it gets ridiculously busy in summer. Dolphin swims and cruises are popular, and the trip to Queenscliff on the ferry is a fun outing. The small Sorrento Beach Information

---

BUCKLEY'S CHANCE

In October 1803 William Buckley (1780–1856), a strapping 6ft 7in bricklayer, was transported to Victoria's first settlement (now Sorrento) as a convict for receiving stolen goods.

Buckley and three others escaped in December, though one was shot dead during the escape. The remaining three set off around the bay, thinking they were heading to Sydney, but two turned back and died from lack of food and water.

Buckley wandered for weeks, surviving on shellfish and berries. He was on his last legs when two Wathaurong women found him, and Buckley spent the next 32 years living with the nomadic clan on the Bellarine Peninsula, learning their customs and language.

In 1835 Buckley surrendered to a party from a survey ship. He was almost unable to speak English, and the startled settlers dubbed him the 'Wild White Man'. Buckley was subsequently pardoned and acted as an interpreter and mediator between white settlers and the Wathaurong people. John Morgan's 1852 book *The Life & Adventures of William Buckley* provides an insight into Aboriginal life before white settlement.

The Australian colloquialism 'Buckley's chance' (a very slim or no chance) is said to be based on William Buckley's story, but there's dispute about this. Some claim the expression gained currency in the late 1800s and derived from the name of the Melbourne department store Buckley's & Nunn ('You've got two chances – Buckley's and none').

Centre (☑03-5984 1478; cnr Ocean Beach Rd & George Sts; ☺10am-4pm) is on the main street.

◉ Sights & Activities

The calm bay beach is good for families and you can hire paddle boards on the foreshore. At low tide, the rock pool at the back beach is a safe spot for adults and children to swim and snorkel, and the surf beach is patrolled in summer. The 10-minute climb up to Coppins Lookout offers good views.

Historic Buildings   NOTABLE BUILDINGS

The grand 19th-century buildings constructed from locally quarried limestone, including the Hotel Sorrento (1871), Continental Hotel (1875) and Koonya Hotel (1878), look fabulous in the late-afternoon sun.

Collins Settlement
Historic Site   HISTORIC SITE

(Leggett Way; ☺1.30-4pm Sat & Sun) Apart from four graves that are believed to hold the remains of 30 original settlers, there's little evidence of Sorrento's original abandoned settlement. The Collins Settlement Historic Site, midway between Sorrento and Blairgowrie, marks the 1803 settlement site at Sullivan Bay, and a display centre tells its story.

Sorrento Museum   MUSEUM

(☑03-5984 0255; 827 Melbourne Rd; adult/child $5/free; ☺1.30-4.30pm Sat, Sun & public/school holidays) Sorrento Museum has interesting displays on the early history of Sorrento and Portsea, and a pioneer garden.

☞ Tours

★Moonraker Charters   SWIMMING
See p37.

★Polperro Dolphin Swims   SWIMMING
See p37.

Sorrento Tours   BOAT TOUR

(☑1300 996 434; www.adventuresails.com.au; adult/child $38/25; ☺12.30pm & 2.30pm) Sightseeing tours aboard a catamaran. Also sunset sails ($80 per person).

🛏 Sleeping

Sorrento Foreshore
Camping Ground   CAMPGROUND $

(☑03-5950 1011; Nepean Hwy; unpowered/powered sites $26/35, peak season $41/46; ☺Nov-May) Hilly, bush-clad sites between the bay beach and the main road into Sorrento.

Sorrento Beach
House YHA   HOSTEL $

(☑03-5984 4323; www.sorrento-beachhouse.com; 3 Miranda St; dm/d from $30/90) This purpose-built hostel situated in a quiet but central location maintains a relaxed atmosphere – the back deck and garden are great places to catch up with other travellers. Staff can also organise horse riding, snorkelling and diving trips.

Carmel of Sorrento   GUESTHOUSE $$

(☑03-5984 3512; www.carmelofsorrento.com.au; 142 Ocean Beach Rd, Sorrento; d $130-220) This lovely old limestone house, right in the centre of Sorrento, has been tastefully restored in period style and neatly marries the town's history with contemporary comfort. There are three Edwardian-style suites with bathrooms and continental breakfast, and two modern self-contained units.

GLENN VAN DER KNIJFF/GETTY IMAGES ©

Whitehall Guesthouse

Whitehall Guesthouse
& Oceanic Apartments
B&B, APARTMENTS **$$**

(☑ 03-5984 4166; www.oceanicgroup.com.au;
235 Ocean Beach Rd; d $130-290, apt $200-290;
✳ ☎) This gracious limestone two-storey
guesthouse on the road to the back beach
has dreamy views from its timber verandah,
though most rooms are small and old-style
with shared bathrooms down the hall – the
rooms with bathrooms are more spacious.
Across the road, Oceanic Apartments ditch
the period charm with spruce self-contained,
split-level apartments.

Hotel Sorrento
HOTEL **$$$**

(☑ 03-5984 2206; www.hotelsorrento.com.au;
5-15 Hotham Rd, Sorrento; motel r $195-280, apt
$220-320) The legendary Hotel Sorrento is
well known as a pub and restaurant but it
also has some slick accommodation. The
motel-style Heritage and Garden suites are
modern and well appointed, but the On the
Hill apartments are the ones to go for, with
airy living spaces, spacious bathrooms, private balconies, spas and bay views. The hotel
has its own spa centre.

✕ Eating & Drinking

Sorrento's main street, Ocean Beach Rd, has
most of the town's cafes and restaurants,
with tables and chairs spilling out along the
footpaths in summer. The town's three pubs,
the historic Hotel Sorrento, Continental Hotel and Koonya Hotel are all good places for

a meal or drink, and all have live music in
summer.

Stringer's
CAFE, DELI **$**

(☑ 03-5984 2010; 2 Ocean Beach Rd; light meals
$4-9; ⊙ 8am-2.30pm) Stringer's is a Sorrento
institution with thoughtfully prepared sand-
wiches, snacks and light meals. If it has the
egg, bacon and chive tart for breakfast, you've
hit the jackpot.

Sisters
CAFE **$**

(☑ 03-5984 4646; 151 Ocean Beach Rd; mains $12-
20; ⊙ 8am-4pm Mon, Tue, Thu & Fri, to 5pm Sat &
Sun) The dishes at this gorgeous courtyard
cafe burst with goodness, whether it's the
eggplant parmigiana, chickpea salad or the
frangipani tart.

The Baths
FISH & CHIPS **$**

(☑ 03-5984 1500; www.thebaths.com.au; 3278
Point Nepean Rd, Sorrento; fish & chips $10, restau-
rant mains $27-36; ⊙ noon-8pm) The waterfront
deck of the former sea baths is the perfect
spot for lunch or a romantic sunset dinner
overlooking the jetty and the Queenscliff ferry. The menu has some good seafood choices
and there's a popular takeaway fish and chip-
pery at the front.

Smokehouse
ITALIAN **$$**

(☑ 03-5984 1246; 182 Ocean Beach Rd, Sorrento;
mains $20-34; ⊙ 6-9pm) Gourmet pizzas and
pastas are the speciality at this local family
favourite. Innovative toppings and the aro-

mas wafting from the wood-fired oven hint at the key to its success.

Acquolina Ristorante
ITALIAN $$

(☑03-5984 0811; 26 Ocean Beach Rd; mains $26-36; ☺6-10pm Thu-Mon, daily in summer, closed Jun-Sep) Acquolina set the bar when it opened in Sorrento with its authentic northern-Italian fare. This is hearty, simple food – handmade pasta and ravioli dishes matched with imported Italian wines and homemade (utterly irresistible) tiramisu.

Loquat
MODERN AUSTRALIAN $$

(☑03-5984 4444; www.loquat.com.au; 3183 Point Nepean Rd; 2-course meal from $30, mains $30-38) An in-crowd frequents this trendily converted cottage, but its staying power is due to excellent food – everything from fish and chips to chargrilled quail.

Portsea
POP 446

The last village on the peninsula is Portsea, where many from Melbourne's establishment have built seaside mansions. The Farnsworth Track (1.5km, 30 minutes) will take you out to scenic London Bridge, a natural rock formation, where you can spot middens of the Boonwurrung people who once called this area home.

Bayplay (☑03-5984 0888; www.bayplay.com.au; 3755 Point Nepean Rd) offers aquatic activities and tours (PADI courses, snorkelling and sea kayaking) and hires equipment (kayaks four/eight hours $50/80), and Dive Victoria (see p39) runs diving and snorkelling trips.

Portsea's heart is the Portsea Hotel (☑03-5984 2213; www.portseahotel.com.au; Point Nepean Rd, Portsea; s/d without bathroom from $75/105, s/d with bathroom from $135/175), a huge pub with an excellent bistro (mains $24 to $39) and old-style accommodation (most rooms have shared bathrooms) that increases in price based on sea views (weekend rates are higher).

LIQUID LUNCH

Most of the peninsula's wineries are in the hills between Red Hill and Merricks, and most have excellent cafes or restaurants attached. Several companies offer winery tours – ask at the Peninsula Visitor Information Centre (☑03-5987 3078, 1800 804 009; www.visitmorningtonpeninsula.org; 359b Nepean Hwy, Dromana; ☺9am-5pm).

Wineries to consider include the following:

Montalto (☑03-5989 8412; www.montalto.com.au; 33 Shoreham Rd, Red Hill South; cafe mains $14-18, restaurant mains $35-39; ☺cellar door 11am-5pm, cafe noon-4pm Sat & Sun, restaurant noon-3pm daily, 6.30-11pm Fri & Sat) Montalto is one of the Mornington Peninsula's best winery restaurants, and the pinot noir and chardonnay here are terrific. There's also the piazza and garden cafe for casual dining, as well as an olive grove and shop.

Port Phillip Estate (☑03-5989 4444; www.portphillipestate.com.au; 263 Red Hill Rd, Red Hill South; 2-/3-course meal from $68/85, cellar door mains $15-22; ☺cellar door 11am-5pm, restaurant noon-3pm Wed-Sun, 6.30-9pm Fri & Sat) Home of Port Phillip Estate and Kooyong wines, this award-winning winery has an excellent, breezy restaurant and some lighter cellar-door meals.

Red Hill Estate (☑03-5931 0177; www.redhillestate.com.au; 53 Shoreham Rd, Red Hill South; ☺cellar door 11am-5pm, restaurant noon-5pm daily, 6.30-11pm Fri & Sat) Red Hill Estate's signature pinot noir and sparkling wines are outstanding, while Max's Restaurant is one of the best on the peninsula.

Ten Minutes by Tractor (☑03-5989 6080; www.tenminutesbytractor.com.au; 1333 Mornington-Flinders Rd, Main Ridge; 5-/8-course tasting menu $109/139, 2-/3-course meal $69/89; ☺cellar door 11am-5pm, restaurant noon-3pm Wed-Sun, 6.30-9pm Thu-Sat) This is one of regional Victoria's best restaurants and you won't find a better wine list on the peninsula. The name comes from the three vineyards, which are each 10 minutes apart by tractor.

T'Gallant (☑03-5989 6565; www.tgallant.com.au; 1385 Mornington-Flinders Rd, Main Ridge; mains $16-32; ☺cellar door 9am-5pm, restaurant noon-3pm Mon-Fri, 11.30am-4pm Sat & Sun) This winery pioneered luscious pinot gris in Australia and produces the country's best. There's fine dining at La Baracca Trattoria and sometimes live music on weekends.

Mornington Peninsula National Park

This national park showcases some of the peninsula's most scenic and isolated spots, although it is well known to the surfers, hikers and fisherfolk who have their secret spots along the 26km from Portsea to Cape Schanck. For the less actively inclined, there are also barbecue facilities, lookouts and birdwatching tours available.

If you want to learn to surf, contact East Coast Surf School (☑0417 526 465, 03-5989 2198; www.eastcoastsurfschool.net.au; 226 Balnarring Rd, Merricks North; lessons per person $55) or Mornington Peninsula Surf School (☑0417 338 079; www.greenroomsurf.com.au; 6 Chetwyn Ct, Frankston South; group/private lessons $55/150).

You can ride a horse along Gunnamatta Beach with Gunnamatta Trail Rides (☑03-5988 6755; www.gunnamatta.com.au; 150 Sandy Rd, Fingal; rides per person $70-120) on excursions ranging from half an hour to a full day.

Built in 1859, Cape Schanck Lightstation (☑03-5988 6184; www.capeschancklighthouse.com.au; 420 Cape Schanck Rd; museum only adult/child/family $13.50/9.50/37, museum & lighthouse $16.50/10.50/44; ⊙10.30am-4pm) is a photogenic working lighthouse with a kiosk, a museum, information centre and regular guided tours. You can stay at Cape Schanck B&B (☑1300 885 259; www.capeschancklighthouse.com.au; 420 Cape Schanck Rd; d from $130) in the limestone Keeper's Cottage.

From the light station, descend the steps of the boardwalk that leads to the craggy cape for outstanding views. Longer walks include tracks to Bushrangers Bay, which can be approached from Cape Schanck or the Bushrangers Bay car park on Boneo Rd (C777) – 5km return. Wild Fingal Beach is a 6km return walk.

Flinders

POP 622

Flinders is a delightful, relaxed community, home to a busy fishing fleet. It has also been drawing in the surfing crowd for decades, while golfers know the cliff-top Flinders Golf Club (p102) course as the most scenic, and wind blown, in Victoria.

The historic Flinders Hotel (☑03-5989 0201; www.flindershotel.com.au; cnr Cook & Wood Sts; d $225-500; ✱) provides modern, well-equipped motel units. For meals there's the indoor-outdoor Deck Bar Bistro (mains $18-36; ⊙noon-3pm & 5.30-9pm) where pub grub goes gastronomic – nothing too fussy, just staple dishes such as steak and parma done really well – or the celebrated fine-dining experience of Terminus (2-/3-course meal $69/89; ⊙6-10pm Fri, noon-2.30pm & 6-10pm Sat, noon-2.30pm Sun).

French Island

POP 116

Isolated and windswept, French Island retains a real sense of peace although its history shows a much more tumultuous past, having served as a penal settlement for prisoners serving out their final years from 1916. You can still visit the original prison farm.

MORNINGTON PENINSULA FLINDERS

OFF THE BEATEN TRACK

POINT NEPEAN NATIONAL PARK

The peninsula's tip is marked by the scenic Point Nepean National Park (http://parkweb.vic.gov.au; Point Nepean Rd), originally a quarantine station and army base. A large section of the park is a former range area and is still out of bounds due to unexploded ordnance, but there's plenty to see here and long stretches of traffic-free road that make for excellent cycling. There are also plenty of walking trails throughout the park and at the tip is Fort Nepean, which played an important role in Australian defence from the 1880s to 1945. On the parade ground are two historic gun barrels that fired the first Allied shots in WWI and WWII. Quarantine is a legendary surf break at the Rip, and is still only accessible by boat.

Point Nepean Visitor Information Centre (☑03-5984 6014; Point Nepean Rd; ⊙9am-6pm Jan, to 5pm Feb-Apr & Oct-Dec, 10am-5pm May-Sep) will give you the lowdown on the park and hires bikes for $25 per day. You can walk or cycle to the point (12km return), or take the shuttle bus (adult/child return $10/7.50), a hop-on, hop-off bus service that departs the visitor centre six times daily.

Flinders front beach

The island is accessible only by ferry, which docks at Tankerton; from there it's around 2km to the licensed French Island General Store (see p41), which also serves as post office, and tourist-information and bike-hire centre, and has accommodation ($120 per person). Bikes can also be hired at Tankerton Jetty.

Located 10km from Tankerton is the Bayview Chicory Kilns (Bayview Rd; ⊙ daily), where fourth-generation local Lois will give you a tour of the historic kilns (by donation), show you a few resident koalas and whip up chicory coffee and Devonshire teas in her rustic cafe. Chicory (a coffee substitute) was the island's biggest industry from 1897 to 1963. You can camp here for $8/5 per adult/child.

☞ Tours

If you want to see the best of the island, especially if your time is limited, a tour is the best way to go. Book ahead and arrange a pick up from Tankerton Jetty.

French Island Biosphere Bus Tours   BUS TOUR
(☏ 0412 671 241, 03-5980 1241; www.frenchisland-tours.com.au; half-day adult/child $25/12, full day $49/22; ⊙ Tue, Thu, Sun, plus Sat during school holidays) Lois from the Bayview Chicory Kilns runs half-day tours with morning or afternoon tea. The full-day tour includes lunch. The ferry to the island costs extra.

🛏 Sleeping

Fairhaven   CAMPGROUND
(☏ 03-5986 9100; www.parkweb.vic.gov.au) FREE
On the western shore where the wetlands meet the ocean, this camping ground provides a real getaway experience, with sites offering little more than a compost toilet. Bookings essential.

Tortoise Head Lodge   B&B $
(☏ 03-5980 1234; www.tortoisehead.net; 10 Tankerton Rd, Tankerton; budget s/d/f $60/90/120, cabins s/d $90/130) A short stroll from the ferry, this has knock-out water views and is great value.

McLeod Eco Farm   GUESTHOUSE $
(☏ 03-5980 1224; www.mcleodecofarm.com; McLeod Rd; per person with breakfast & dinner $98) ✿
Formerly the island's prison, this organic farm offers cosy guesthouse rooms (former officers' quarters) and makes abundant use of recycled furniture. All rooms have shared bathrooms. The meals here are outstanding.

❶ Getting There & Around

Inter Island Ferries (☏ 03-9585 5730; www.interislandferries.com.au) runs a service between Stony Point and Tankerton (10 minutes, at least two daily, four on Tue, Thu, Sat & Sun, adult/child return $24/12).

You can hire bikes ($25 per day) from the kiosk at the jetty in summer and from the general store.

Goldfields

Victoria's heartland is full of gorgeous country towns offering some of the best food and drink options in the state. And that's not the only gold in the hills...

Woodend

POP 5400

This pleasant town 13km from Mt Macedon is easily reached by train from Melbourne (70km away) and makes a popular base for road cyclists and mountain-bikers exploring the Macedon Ranges. It's also the gateway to Hanging Rock and the wineries in the region.

Woodend
TOM COCKREM/GETTY IMAGES ©

✗ Eating & Drinking

Village Larder   CAFE **$$**

(☑ 03-5427 3399; www.thevillagelarder.com.au; 81 High St; mains $12-24; ⊙ 8am-4pm daily, & 6-10pm Sat) There's retro style at the Village Larder, where local organic produce is crafted into dishes with a hearty Modern British twist.

★ Holgate Brewhouse   PUB

(☑ 03-5427 2510; www.holgatebrewhouse.com; 79 High St; d $135-185; mains $19-29; ⊙ noon-late) The excellent Holgate Brewhouse, at Keatings Hotel, is a cracking brewery pub producing a range of hand-pumped European-style ales and lagers on site. Serves hearty Mod Oz bistro food and has pub accommodation upstairs.

ℹ Information

Woodend Visitor Centre (☑ 03-5427 2033; www.visitmacedonranges.com; High St; ⊙ 9am-5pm)

Hanging Rock

Hanging Rock, a series of volcanic rock formations, is said to be one, if not the, best example in the world of a volcanic plug (mamelon).

A sacred site of the traditional owners, the Wurundjeri people, you're welcome to clamber up the rocks, with lookout names including Stonehenge, McDonald's Look-out and the Eagle, along the 20-minute path. The walk-through Hanging Rock Discovery Centre explains its history and geology, and there's a cafe next door. Guided night walks operate in summer months; call to book on ☑ 03-5421 1469. Below the rock is a cricket ground where you can see kangaroos and its famous racecourse (www.hangingrockracingclub.com.au), which hosts two excellent picnic race meetings, on New Year's Day and Australia Day. It's also a venue for 'A Day on the Green' concerts, hosting big-name acts from the Rolling Stones to Leonard Cohen.

❶ Information

Hanging Rock is located approximately 80km (1 hour) to the north of Melbourne and can be accessed from the A79 Calder Freeway.

Kyneton

POP 4460

Kyneton was the main coach stop between Melbourne and Bendigo, and the centre for the farmers who supplied the diggings with fresh produce. Today, Piper St is a historic precinct lined with bluestone buildings that have been transformed into cafes, antique shops, museums and restaurants.

◎ Sights

Kyneton Historical Museum   MUSEUM
See p46.

🎉 Festivals & Events

Kyneton Daffodil & Arts Festival   CARNIVAL
(www.kynetondaffodilarts.org.au; ⊙ Sep) Kyneton is renowned for its daffodils. The annual Kyneton Daffodil & Arts Festival has 10 days of gala evenings, markets, concerts, fairs and art and flower shows.

Budburst   FOOD, WINE
(☑ 1800 244 711; www.macedonrangeswine.com.au/budburst-festival/; ⊙ mid-Nov) Budburst is a wine and food festival hosted at wineries throughout the Macedon Ranges over several days.

🛏 Sleeping & Eating

Kyneton's eat street is historic Piper St, with a fabulous cafe and restaurant scene.

Airleigh-Rose Cottage   B&B $$$
(☑ 0402 783 489; www.airleighrosecottage.com.au; 10 Begg St; r 2 nights $490, min 2-night stay) Attractive wood-and-brick rooms in a Federation-era cottage.

★ Mr Carsisi   MIDDLE EASTERN $$$
(☑ 03-5422 3769; http://mrcarsisi.com; 37c Piper St; mains $29-39; ⊙ 11.30am-late Fri-Tue) Turkish tastes and Middle Eastern mezze dominate this well-regarded place, which does a faultless job of combining foreign flavours with local produce – the honey-and-cardamom Milawa duck breast is typical of the genre.

Annie Smithers Bistrot   MODERN AUSTRALIAN $$$
(☑ 03-5422 2039; www.anniesmithers.com.au; 72 Piper St; mains $36-40; ⊙ noon-2.30pm & 6-9pm Thu-Sat, noon-2.30pm Sun) One of central Victoria's most exciting new restaurants, this fine place has a menu that changes with the seasons, dish descriptions that read like a culinary short story about regional produce and carefully conceived taste combinations – such as hazelnut and fennel seed crumbed cutlet of pork, apple and fennel puree, spring 'slaw, and pork and cider jus.

❶ Information

Kyneton Visitor Centre (☑ 1800 244 711, 03-5422 6110; www.visitmacedonranges.com; 127 High St; ⊙ 9am-5pm) On the southeastern entry to town. Ask for the Town Walks, Self Drive Tour and Campaspe River Walk brochures.

❶ Getting There & Away

Kyneton is just off the Calder Hwy about 90km northwest of Melbourne.

Castlemaine

POP 9124

At the heart of the central Victorian goldfields, Castlemaine is a rewarding working-class town where a growing community of artists and tree-changers. The main grid of streets is home to some stirring examples of late-19th-century architecture.

History

After gold was discovered at Specimen Gully in 1851, the Mt Alexander Diggings attracted some 30,000 diggers and Castlemaine became the thriving marketplace for the goldfields. The town's importance waned as the surface gold was exhausted by the 1860s but,

When gold was discovered in New South Wales in May 1851, a reward was offered to anyone who could find gold within 300km of Melbourne, amid fears that Victoria would be left behind. They needn't have worried. By June a significant discovery was made at Clunes, 32km north of Ballarat, and prospectors flooded into central Victoria.

Over the next few months, fresh gold finds were made almost weekly around Victoria. Then in September 1851 the greatest gold discovery ever known was made at Moliagul, followed by others at Ballarat, Bendigo, Mt Alexander and many more. By the end of 1851 hopeful miners were coming from England, Ireland, Europe, China and the failing goldfields of California. While the gold rush had its tragic side (including epidemics that swept through the camps), plus its share of rogues (including bushrangers who attacked the gold shipments), it ushered in a fantastic era of growth and prosperity for Victoria. Within 12 years the population had increased from 77,000 to 540,000. Mining companies invested heavily in the region, the development of roads and railways accelerated and huge shanty towns were replaced by Victoria's modern provincial cities, most notably Ballarat, Bendigo and Castlemaine, which reached the height of their splendour in the 1880s.

The world's largest alluvial nugget, the 72kg Welcome Stranger, was found in Moliagul in 1869, while the 27kg Hand of Faith (the largest nugget found with a metal detector) was found near Kingower in 1980.

fortunately, the centre of town was well established by then and remains relatively intact.

Sights & Activities

★ Castlemaine Art Gallery & Historical Museum
GALLERY, MUSEUM

(☎03-5472 2292; www.castlemainegallery.com; 14 Lyttleton St; adult/student/child $4/3/free; ◎10am-5pm) A superb art deco building houses this gallery, which features colonial and contemporary Australian art, including works by well-known Australian artists such as Frederick McCubbin and Russell Drysdale. The museum, in the basement, provides an insight into local history, with costumes, china and gold-mining relics.

Castlemaine Botanical Gardens
GARDENS

These majestic gardens, one of the oldest in Victoria (established 1860), strike a perfect balance between sculpture and wild bush among awe-inspiring National Trust–registered trees and the artificial Lake Joanna.

Burke & Wills Monument
MONUMENT

(Wills St) For a good view over town, head up to the Burke and Wills Monument on Wills St (follow Lyttleton St east of the centre). Robert O'Hara Burke was a police superintendent in Castlemaine before his fateful trek.

Victorian Goldfields Railway
TRAIN

(☎03-5470 6658; www.vgr.com.au; adult/child return $45/20) This historic steam train heads

through the box-ironbark forests of Victoria's gold country, running between Castlemaine and Maldon up to three times a week.

Festivals & Events

Castlemaine State Festival
ART

(www.castlemainefestival.com.au; ◎Mar-Apr) One of Victoria's leading arts events, featuring theatre, music, art and dance. Held in March or April in odd-numbered years.

Festival of Gardens
GARDEN

(www.festivalofgardens.org; ◎Nov) Over 50 locals open their properties to the public. Held in even-numbered years.

Sleeping

Bookings are essential during festival times, so make use of the area's free accommodation booking service (☎1800 171 888; www.maldoncastlemaine.com).

Castlemaine Gardens Caravan Park
CARAVAN PARK $

(☎03-5472 1125; www.castlemaine-gardens-caravan-park.vic.big4.com.au; Doran Ave; powered/unpowered sites $37/32, cabins $85-155) Beautifully situated next to the botanical gardens and public swimming pool, this leafy park has a camp kitchen, barbecues and recreation hut.

★ Apple Annie's
APARTMENTS $$

(☎03-5472 5311; www.appleannies.com.au; 31 Templeton St; apt $120-160) Beautifully appointed apartments with rustic wooden floorboards,

GOLDFIELDS CASTLEMAINE

pastel shades, open fireplaces and (in the front apartment) a lovely private patio.

Midland Private Hotel GUESTHOUSE **$$**
(📞 0487 198 931; www.themidland.com.au; 2 Templeton St; d $150) Opposite the train station, this lace-decked 1879 hotel is mostly original, so the rooms are old fashioned, but it has plenty of charm, from the art deco entrance to the magnificent guest lounge and attached Maurocco Bar. No children.

✕ Eating

Apple Annie's BAKERY, CAFE **$**
(📞 03-5472 5311; www.appleannies.com.au; 31 Templeton St; mains $10-17; ☺ 8am-4pm Wed-Sat, to 3pm Sun) For freshly baked bread, feta and zucchini fritters or filled baguettes, it's hard to beat this country-style cafe and bakery.

Good Table EUROPEAN **$$**
(📞 03-5472 4400; www.thegoodtable.com.au; 233 Barker St; mains $26-32, 2-/3-course dinner set menu Mon-Thu $25/30; ☺ noon-2pm Thu-Sun, from 6pm daily) In a lovely corner hotel, the Good Table does it well with a thoughtful European-influenced menu that changes regularly in keeping with seasons and fresh market produce. A good wine list is another highlight.

★ Public Inn MODERN AUSTRALIAN **$$$**
(📞 03-5472 3568; www.publicinn.com.au; 165 Barker St; 2-course lunch $39, mains $19-45; ☺ noon-late Fri-Sun, 4pm-late Mon-Thu) The former Criterion Hotel has been brilliantly transformed into a slick bar and restaurant that, with its plush tones and leather couches, wouldn't look out of place in Manhattan. Food is high-end 'gastropub'. Check out the 'barrel wall', where local wines are dispensed.

☆ Entertainment

Bridge Hotel LIVE MUSIC
See p47.

Theatre Royal CINEMA
(📞 03-5472 1196; www.theatreroyal.info; 28 Hargreaves St; cinema tickets adult/child $15.50/12) A theatre since the 1850s, this is a fabulous entertainment venue – classic cinema (dine while watching a movie), touring live performers, a bar and a cafe. Check the program on the website.

ℹ Information

Castlemaine Visitor Centre (📞 03-5471 1795; www.maldoncastlemaine.com; 44 Mostyn St; ☺ 9am-5pm) In the magnificent old Castlemaine Market, a building fronted with a classical Roman-basilica facade, complete with a statue of Ceres, the Roman goddess of the harvest, on top.

Maldon

POP 1236

These days Maldon's town centre, consisting of High St and Main St, is lined with an array of quirky, cute antique stores, cafes, old toy shops, bookshops and local pubs. However,

Castlemaine Art Gallery

evidence of its mining days can be seen all around town

◉ Sights & Activities

Old Post Office
HISTORIC BUILDING

(95 High St) The Old Post Office, built in 1870, was the childhood home of local author Henry Handel Richardson. She (yes, she!) writes about it in her autobiography, *Myself When Young* (1948).

Carman's Tunnel
HISTORIC SITE

(☑ 03-5475 2656; off Parkin's Reef Rd; adult/child $7.50/2.50; ☺ tours 1.30pm, 2.30pm & 3.30pm Sat & Sun, daily in school holidays) For a hands-on experience, Carman's Tunnel is a 570m-long mine tunnel that was excavated in the 1880s and took two years to dig, yet produced only $300 worth of gold. Now you can descend with a guide for a 45-minute candlelit tour.

Mt Tarrengower
VIEWPOINT

Don't miss the 3km drive up to Mt Tarrengower for panoramic views from the poppethead lookout.

Victorian Goldfields Railway
TRAIN

(☑ 03-5470 6658; www.vgr.com.au; adult/child return $45/20) This beautifully restored steam train runs along the original line through the Muckleford forest to Castlemaine (and back) up to three times a week. For a little extra, go 1st class in an oak-lined viewing carriage. The Maldon train station dates from 1884.

✯✯ Festivals & Events

Maldon Folk Festival
MUSIC

(www.maldonfolkfestival.com; 2-day ticket $115; ☺ Oct-Nov) Maldon's main event, this four-day festival attracts dozens of performers, who provide a wide variety of world music at venues around town and at the main stage at Mt Tarrengower Reserve.

⛏ Sleeping & Eating

There are plenty of self-contained cottages and charming B&Bs in restored buildings around town. Try the accommodation booking service (p108).

★ Maldon Miners Cottages
COTTAGE $$

(☑ 0413 541 941; www.heritagecottages.com.au; 41 High St; cottages from $150) Books accommodation in Maldon's 19th-century heritage cottages – a great choice.

Gold Exchange Cafe
CAFE $

(www.goldexchangecafe.com; 44 Main St; meals $7-15; ☺ 9am-5pm Wed-Sun) This tiny licensed cafe is worth a visit for the yabby pies, made from locally farmed yabbies.

ℹ Information

Maldon Visitor Centre (☑ 03-5475 2569; www.maldoncastlemaine.com; 95 High St; ☺ 9am-5pm) Has internet access. Pick up the *Information Guide* and the *Historic Town Walk* brochure, which guides you past some of the town's most historic buildings.

Maryborough

Maryborough is part of central Victoria's 'Golden Triangle', where prospectors still turn up a nugget or two. The town's pride and joy is the magnificent railway station, and now that passenger trains are running here again from Melbourne, it's worth a day trip. Currently there's one direct train a day from Melbourne ($29, 2¼ hours), with others going via Geelong, Ballarat or Castlemaine by bus.

◉ Sights & Activities

Maryborough Railway Station
HISTORIC BUILDING

See p48.

Worsley Cottage
MUSEUM

(☑ 03-5461 2518; www.vicnet.net.au/~mbhs; 3 Palmerston St; adult/child $5/1; ☺ 10am-noon Tue & Thu, 2-4pm Sun) Built in 1894, Worsley Cottage is the local historical society museum. Every room is furnished with pieces from the times, often donated by local people, and there's a large photographic collection. Records held here are used in family history research.

Coiltek Gold Centre
PROSPECTING

See p48.

✯✯ Festivals & Events

Highland Gathering
SCOTTISH

(www.maryboroughhighlandsociety.com; ☺ 1 Jan) Have a fling at Maryborough's Scottish festival, with races, stalls, tossing the caber and highland music; held every New Year's Day since 1857 (except during World War II).

⛏ Sleeping & Eating

There's plenty of accommodation in the region. Contact Central Goldfields visitor centre or browse its website. High St is the foodie area, with cafes, restaurants, bakeries, takeaways, pubs and clubs.

Maryborough

Caravan Park
CAMPGROUND $

(📞 03-5460 4848; www.maryboroughcaravanpark. com.au; 7-9 Holyrood St; unpowered/powered sites $22/27, bunkhouse dm $25, cabins $75-95; ✱ ▣) Close to the town centre and nicely located beside Lake Victoria, the caravan park is well set up, with Maryborough's cheapest accommodation.

Station Cafe
CAFE $$

(📞 03-5461 4683; www.stationantiques.com.au; 38c Victoria St; mains $14-31; ⊙10am-4pm Mon & Wed-Fri, 9.30am-4.30pm Sat & Sun) This excellent cafe is in a lovely light-filled room in the grand Maryborough train station. Stop in for a coffee or speciality crêpe. The dining menu features pasta and Black Angus steaks.

ℹ Information

Central Goldfields Visitor Centre (📞 03-5460 4511, 1800 356 511; www.visitmaryborough. com.au; cnr Alma & Nolan Sts; ⊙9am-5pm; @) Loads of helpful maps and friendly staff. There's also a replica of the famous Welcome Stranger gold nugget here, and internet access and a library in the same complex.

Ballarat

POP 85,935

Ballarat was built on gold and it's easy to see the proceeds of those days in the grand Victorian-era architecture around the city centre. The single biggest attraction here is the fabulous, re-created gold-mining village at Sovereign Hill, but there's plenty more in this busy provincial city to keep you occupied, including grand gold-mining-era architecture and a stunning new museum dedicated to the Eureka Stockade. Rug up if you visit in the winter months – Ballarat is renowned for being chilly.

History

The area around here was known to the local indigenous population as 'Ballaarat', meaning 'resting place'. When gold was discovered here in August 1851, giving irresistible momentum to the central Victorian gold rush that had begun two months earlier in Clunes, thousands of diggers flooded in, forming a shanty town of tents and huts. Ballarat's alluvial goldfields were the tip of the golden iceberg, and when deep shaft mines were sunk they struck incredibly rich quartz reefs.

In 1854 the Eureka Rebellion pitted miners against the government and put Ballarat at the forefront of miners' rights.

◉ Sights & Activities

Take the time to walk along **Lydiard St**, one of Australia's finest streetscapes for Victorian-era architecture. Impressive buildings include **Her Majesty's Theatre** (📞 03-53335888; www.hermaj.com; 17 Lydiard St Sth), **Craig's Royal Hotel** (📞 03-5331 1377; www.craigsroyal.com; 10 Lydiard St South; d $230-450), **George Hotel** (📞 03-5333 4866; www.georgehotelballarat.com. au; 27 Lydiard St Nth; d/f/ste from $145/220/260; ✱ 🛜) and the **art gallery**. The main drag, impressive **Sturt St**, had to be three chains wide (60m) to allow for the turning circle of bullock wagons.

★ Sovereign Hill
HISTORIC SITE

(📞 03-5337 1100; www.sovereignhill.com.au; Bradshaw St; adult/child/student/family $49.50/22/39.60/122; ⊙10am-5pm, to 5.30pm during daylight saving) You'll need to set aside at least half a day to visit this fascinating recreation of an 1860s gold-mining township. The site was mined in the gold-rush era and much of the equipment is original, as is the mine shaft. Kids love panning for gold in the stream, watching the hourly gold pour and exploring the old-style lolly shop.

The main street here is a living history museum, with people performing their chores dressed in costumes of the time. Sovereign Hill opens again at night for the impressive sound-and-light show, **Blood on the Southern Cross** (📞 03-5337 1199; adult/child/student/family $59/31.50/47.20/160, combined with Sovereign Hill ticket $107.50/53.50/86/282), a dramatic simulation of the Eureka Stockade battle.

ℹ BALLARAT PASS

The **Ballarat Pass** (📞 1800 446 633; www.visitballarat.com.au/things-to-do/ballarat-pass; adult 3/4-attraction pass $96/107, child $51/58, family $257/288), a three-attraction pass, covers entry to Sovereign Hill, Kryal Castle and Ballarat Wildlife Park. The four-attraction pass adds in the Museum of Australian Democracy at Eureka. Buying a pass will save you around 10% off the normal entry price. The pass can be bought over the phone or at the Ballarat visitor centre.

GOLDFIELDS BALLARAT

Ballarat

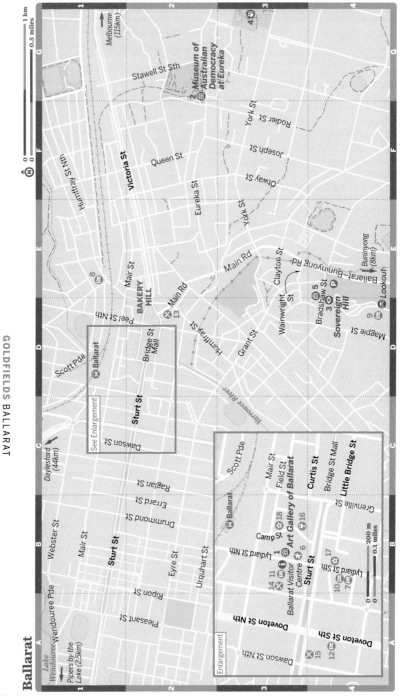

Ballarat

Top Sights
1 Art Gallery of Ballarat.........................B3
2 Museum of Australian
   Democracy at Eureka.....................G2
3 Sovereign Hill D4

Sights
4 Ballarat Wildlife Park G3
5 Gold Museum E4

Activities, Courses & Tours
6 Gold Shop B3

Sleeping
7 Ansonia on Lydiard.............................B4
8 Ballarat Backpackers Hostel...............E1
9 Comfort Inn Sovereign Hill D4
10 Craig's Royal Hotel B4
11 George Hotel B3
12 Oscar's A4

Eating
13 Catfish...D2
14 Forge Pizzeria......................................B3
15 L'Espresso A4

Drinking & Nightlife
16 Haida B3

Entertainment
17 Her Majesty's Theatre.........................B4
18 Karova Lounge B3

There are two shows nightly, but times vary so check in advance; bookings are essential.

Your ticket also gets you into the nearby **Gold Museum** (Bradshaw St; adult/child $11.20/5.90; ⊙9.30am-5.30pm), which sits on a mullock heap from an old mine. There are imaginative displays and samples from all the old mining areas, as well as gold nuggets, coins and a display on the Eureka Rebellion.

★ **Museum of Australian Democracy at Eureka**　　　　MUSEUM
(MADE; ☑1800 287 113; www.made.org; cnr Eureka & Rodier Sts; adult/child/family $12/8/35; ⊙10am-5pm) Standing on the site of the Eureka Rebellion, this fine museum opened in May 2013 and has already established itself as one of Ballarat's top attractions. Taking the Eureka Rebellion as its starting point – pride of place goes to the preserved remnants of the original Eureka flag and multimedia displays re-create the events of 1854 – the museum then broadens out to discuss democracy in Australia and beyond through a series of interactive exhibits.

★ **Art Gallery of Ballarat**　　　　GALLERY
(☑03-5320 5858; www.balgal.com; 40 Lydiard St Nth; ⊙10am-5pm) FREE Established in 1884 and moved to its current location in 1890, the Art Gallery of Ballarat is the oldest provincial gallery in Australia. The architectural gem houses a wonderful collection of early colonial paintings, with works from noted Australian artists (including Tom Roberts, Sir Sidney Nolan, Russell Drysdale and Fred Williams) and contemporary works. Free iPod tours are available and there are free guided tours at 2pm Wednesday to Sunday.

Ballarat Wildlife Park　　　　ZOO
(☑03-5333 5933; www.wildlifepark.com.au; cnr York & Fussell Sts; adult/child/family $28/16/75; ⊙9am-5.30pm, tour 11am) Ballarat's tranquil wildlife park is strong on native fauna, from the sweet little King Island wallabies to Tasmanian devils, emus, quokkas, snakes, eagles and crocs. There's a daily guided tour, and weekend programs include a koala show, wombat show, snake show and crocodile feeding.

Kryal Castle　　　　CASTLE
(☑03-5334 7388; http://kryalcastle.com.au; 121 Forbes Rd, Leigh Creek; adult/child/family $31/19/89; ⊙10am-4pm Sat & Sun, & daily during school holidays) It may be kitsch but the kids will love a day out at this mock medieval castle and self-styled medieval adventure park. Knights and damsels in distress wander the grounds and there's everything from a Dragon's Labyrinth and Wizard's Workshop to jousting re-enactments and a torture dungeon. You can also sleep overnight in one of the semi-luxurious Castle Suites (r from $130).

Gold Shop　　　　GOLD PANNING
(☑03-5333 4242; www.thegoldshop.com.au; 8a Lydiard St North; ⊙10am-5pm Mon-Sat) Hopeful prospectors can pick up miners' rights and rent metal detectors at the Gold Shop in the historic Mining Exchange.

Tours

Eerie Tours　　　　TOUR
(☑1300 856 668; www.eerietours.com.au; adult/child/family $27.50/17.50/75; ⊙8pm or 9pm Wed-Sun) Relive the ghoulish parts of Ballarat's past with a night-time ghost tour or cemetery tour.

Festivals & Events

Begonia Festival　　　　STREET CARNIVAL
(www.ballaratbegoniafestival.com) This 100-year-old festival, held over the Labour Day

GOLDFIELDS BALLARAT

THE EUREKA STOCKADE

On 29 November, 1854, about 800 miners tossed their licences into a bonfire during a mass meeting then, led by Irishman Peter Lalor, built a stockade at Eureka, where they prepared to fight for their rights. A veteran of Italy's independence struggle named Raffaello Carboni called on the crowd, 'irrespective of nationality, religion and colour', to salute the Southern Cross as the 'refuge of all the oppressed from all the countries on Earth'.

On 3 December the government ordered troopers (the mounted colonial police) to attack the stockade. There were only 150 miners within the makeshift barricades and the fight lasted a short but devastating 20 minutes, leaving 25 miners and four troopers dead.

Though the rebellion was short-lived, the miners won the sympathy and support of many Victorians. The government deemed it wise to acquit the leaders of the charge of high treason. It's interesting to note that only four of the miners were Australian born; the others hailed from Ireland, Britain, Italy, Corsica, Greece, Germany, Russia, Holland, France, Switzerland, Spain, Portugal, Sweden, the US, Canada and the West Indies.

The licence fee was abolished and replaced by a Miners' Right, which cost one pound a year. This gave miners the right to search for gold; to fence in, cultivate and build a dwelling on a piece of land; and to vote for members of the Legislative Assembly. The rebel miner Peter Lalor became a member of parliament some years later. Eureka remains a powerful symbol in Australian culture, standing as it does for the treasured notions of workers' rights, democracy and 'a fair go for all'.

Goldfield brotherhood in 1854, sadly, had its limits. The 40,000 miners who arrived from southern China to try their luck on the 'new gold mountain' were often a target of individual violence and systemic prejudice. Still, the Chinese community persevered, and it has to this day been a strong and enduring presence in the city of Melbourne and throughout regional Victoria.

weekend in early March, includes sensational floral displays, a street parade, fireworks, art shows and music.

🛏 Sleeping

Ballarat Backpackers Hostel   HOSTEL **$**
(☑ 0427 440 661; www.ballaratbackpackers.com.au; 81 Humffray St Nth; dm/s/d $30/40/70) In the old Eastern Station Hotel (1862), this refurbished guesthouse is also a decent corner pub with occasional live music. Rooms are simple but fresh and good value.

★ Comfort Inn
Sovereign Hill   HISTORIC HOTEL **$$**
(☑ 03-5337 1159; www.sovereignhill.com.au/comfort-inn-sovereign-hill; 39-41 Magpie St; r $175-195; ❋ 🛜) Formerly known as Sovereign Hill Lodge, this excellent place has bright, modern rooms that are located a stone's throw from Sovereign Hill itself. Ask about its accommodation-and-entertainment packages. Its 'Night in the Museum' package (single/ double $425/695) lets you stay in the Steinfeld's building at the top of Main St within Sovereign Hill itself, where you'll be served by staff in period dress.

★ Oscar's   BOUTIQUE HOTEL **$$**
(☑ 03-5331 1451; www.oscarshotel.com.au; 18 Doveton St; d $150-200, spa room $225; ❋ 🛜) The 13 rooms in this attractive art deco hotel have been tastefully refurbished to include double showers and spas (watch TV from your spa).

Ansonia on Lydiard   B&B **$$**
(☑ 03-5332 4678; www.theansoniaonlydiard.com.au; 32 Lydiard St South; r $125-225; ❋ 🛜) One of Lydiard St's great hotels, the Ansonia exudes calm with its minimalist design, polished floors, dark-wood furnishings and light-filled atrium. Stylish rooms have large-screen TVs and range from studio apartments for two to family suites.

🍴 Eating

L'Espresso   ITALIAN **$**
(☑ 03-5333 1789; 417 Sturt St; mains $11-20; ⏲ 7.30am-6pm Sun-Thu, to 11pm Fri & Sat) A mainstay on Ballarat's cafe scene, this trendy Italian-style place doubles as a record shop – choose from the whopping jazz, blues and world-music selection while you wait for your espresso or Tuscan bean soup.

★Catfish
THAI **$$**

(☑ 03-5331 5248; www.catfishthai.com.au; 42-44 Main Rd; mains $18-34; ⊙ 6pm-late Tue-Sat) Catfish is the kitchen of chef Damien Jones, who made the Lydiard Wine Bar such a treasured local secret. Thai cooking classes only add to what is an increasingly popular package.

Forge Pizzeria
ITALIAN, PIZZA **$$**

(☑ 03-5337 6635; www.theforgepizzeria.com.au; 14 Armstrong St North; pizzas $15-25; ⊙ noon-11pm) Could this be the start of Ballarat's Bendigo-style renaissance? This brick-walled dining area is the city's coolest eating ticket, with outstanding pizzas and Italian dishes and a fine charcuterie board of Italian cured meats.

Pipers by the Lake
CAFE **$$**

(☑ 03-5334 1811; www.pipersbythelake.com.au; 403 Wendouree Pde; mains $19-33; ⊙ 9am-4pm Sat-Thu, 9am-4pm & 6-10pm Fri) The 1890 Lakeside Lodge was designed by WH Piper and today it's a lovely light-filled cafe with huge windows looking out over the lake and an alfresco courtyard. Dishes range from pulled-pork sandwiches to roasted pumpkin, feta and pine nut risotto.

🍷 Drinking & Entertainment

With its large student population, Ballarat has a lively nightlife. There are some fine old pubs around town but most of the entertainment is centred on Lydiard St and the nearby Camp St precinct.

Haida
LOUNGE

(☑ 03-5331 5346; www.haidabar.com; 12 Camp St; ⊙ 5pm-late Wed-Sun) Haida is a loungy two-level bar where you can relax with a cocktail by the open fire or chill out to DJs and live music downstairs.

Karova Lounge
LIVE MUSIC

(☑ 03-5332 9122; www.karovalounge.com; cnr Field & Camp Sts; ⊙ 9pm-late Wed-Sat) Ballarat's best original live-music venue showcases local and touring bands in a grungy, industrial style.

🛍 Shopping

Mill Markets
MARKET

(☑ 03-5334 7877; www.millmarkets.com.au; 9367 Western Hwy; ⊙ 10am-6pm) A little sister of the popular Mill Market at Daylesford, this huge collection of antiques, retro furnishings and knick-knacks is in the old woolsheds.

ℹ Information

Ballarat Visitor Centre (☑ 1800 446 633, 03-5320 5741; www.visitballarat.com.au; 43 Lydiard St North; ⊙ 9am-5pm) Opposite the art gallery.

ROBIN SMITH/GETTY IMAGES ©

Gold-panning, Sovereign Hill (p111)

ROAD TRIP ESSENTIALS

DRIVING IN AUSTRALIA.........117

Driving Licence & Documents..........................117
Insurance 117
Hiring a Car 117
Maps 118
Roads & Conditions 118
Road Rules 119
Fuel 119
Safety 120
Driving in Outback Australia 120

Driving in Australia

With more than 350,000km of paved roads criss-crossing the country, Australia is an infinitely fascinating road movie come to life.

Driving Fast Facts

➡ **Right or left?** Drive on the left

➡ **Legal driving age** 18

➡ **Top speed limit** 110km/h

➡ **Signature car** Holden Commodore

DRIVING LICENCE & DOCUMENTS

To drive in Australia you'll need to hold a current driving licence issued in English from your home country. If the licence isn't in English, you'll also need to carry an International Driving Permit, issued in your home country.

INSURANCE

Third-party insurance With the exception of NSW and Queensland, third-party personal-injury insurance is included in the vehicle registration cost, ensuring that every registered vehicle carries at least minimum insurance (if registering your own car in NSW or Queensland you'll need to arrange this privately). We recommend extending that minimum to at least third-party property insurance – minor collisions can be amazingly expensive.

Rental vehicles When it comes to hire cars, understand your liability in the event of an accident. Rather than risk paying out thousands of dollars, consider taking out comprehensive car insurance or paying an additional daily amount to the rental company for excess reduction (this reduces the excess payable in the event of an accident from between $2000 and $5000 to a few hundred dollars).

Exclusions Be aware that if travelling on dirt roads you usually will not be covered by insurance unless you have a 4WD (read the fine print). Also, many companies' insurance won't cover the cost of damage to glass (including the windscreen) or tyres.

HIRING A CAR

Larger car-rental companies have drop-offs in major cities and towns. Most companies require drivers to be over the age of 21, though in some cases it's 18 and in others 25.

Suggestions to assist in the process:

➡ Read the contract cover to cover.

➡ Bond: some companies may require a signed credit-card slip, others may actually charge your credit card; if this is the case, find out when you'll get a refund.

➡ Ask if unlimited kilometres are included and, if not, what the extra charge per kilometre is.

Road Trip Websites

Australian Bureau of Meteorology (www.bom.gov.au) Weather information.

Green Vehicle Guide (www.greenvehicleguide.gov.au) Rates Australian vehicles based on greenhouse and air-pollution emissions.

Parks Australia (www.environment.gov.au/parks) Info on national parks and reserves.

RACV (Royal Automobile Club of Victoria; 13 72 28; www.racv.com.au)

Tourism Australia (www.australia.com) Main government tourism site.

Vic Roads (www.vicroads.vic.gov.au) Victorian road conditions.

➡ Find out what excess you'll have to pay if you have a prang, and if it can be lowered by an extra charge per day (this option will usually be offered to you whether you ask or not). Check if your personal travel insurance covers you for vehicle accidents and excess.

➡ Check for exclusions (hitting a kangaroo, damage on unsealed roads etc) and whether you're covered on unavoidable unsealed roads (eg accessing camp sites). Some companies also exclude parts of the car from cover, such as the underbelly, tyres and windscreen.

➡ At pick-up inspect the vehicle for any damage. Make a note of anything on the contract before you sign.

➡ Ask about breakdown and accident procedures.

➡ If you can, return the vehicle during business hours and insist on an inspection in your presence.

The usual big international companies all operate in Australia (Avis, Budget, Europcar, Hertz, Thrifty). The following websites offer last-minute discounts and the opportunity to compare rates between the big operators:

➡ www.carhire.com.au

➡ www.drivenow.com.au

➡ www.webjet.com.au

MAPS

Good-quality road and topographical maps are plentiful and readily available around Australia. State motoring organisations are a dependable source of road maps, including road atlases with comprehensive coverage of road networks.

Hema's *Australia Road Atlas* is a good general road atlas covering the entire country, and it also offers a range of smaller fold-out maps on specific destinations.

ROADS & CONDITIONS

Australia's roads are generally in excellent condition, but never discount the possibility of potholes, especially in rural areas which receive heavy truck traffic.

Overtaking Lanes

If you've spent any time in Europe, you'll be underwhelmed by Australia's dearth of dual carriageway roads. Apart from the Hume Fwy connecting Sydney and Melbourne (the inland route, not the coast road), most motorways are restricted to a 100km (or less) radius around major cities. Although there are regular overtaking lanes on many roads and traffic flows generally maintain a reasonable speed, there are times when you'll become frustrated as you wait to pass a slow caravan, truck or old man in a hat out for a Sunday drive. The only sensible response in such circumstances is patience.

Unsealed Roads

At last count, Australia was so vast that it had 466,874km of unsealed roads – that's significantly more than the distance from earth to the moon! While many of these are suitable for 2WD vehicles when conditions are dry, many more are not, and most become treacherous or impassable after even a little rain. Others peter out into the sand. The simple rule is this – never leave the paved road unless you know the road, have checked recent weather conditions and asked locals for their advice.

Toll Roads

Toll roads are restricted to some freeways within major cities such as Melbourne and Sydney. If you're travelling in a rental vehicle, it should have the necessary electronic reader and any tolls will be charged when you return your vehicle. Either way, take

Road Distances (km)

	Adelaide	Albany	Alice Springs	Birdsville	Brisbane	Broome	Cairns	Canberra	Cape York	Darwin	Kalgoorlie	Melbourne	Perth	Sydney	Townsville
Albany	2649														
Alice Springs	1512	3573													
Birdsville	1183	3244	1176												
Brisbane	1942	4178	1849	1573											
Broome	4043	2865	2571	3564	5065										
Cairns	3079	5601	2396	1919	1705	4111									
Canberra	1372	4021	2725	2038	1287	5296	2923								
Cape York	4444	6566	3361	2884	2601	5076	965	3888							
Darwin	3006	5067	1494	2273	3774	1844	2820	3948	3785						
Kalgoorlie	2168	885	3092	2763	3697	3052	5234	3540	6199	4896					
Melbourne	728	3377	2240	1911	1860	4811	3496	637	4461	3734	2896				
Perth	2624	411	3548	3219	4153	2454	6565	3996	7530	4298	598	3352			
Sydney	1597	4246	3109	2007	940	5208	2634	289	3599	3917	3765	862	3869		
Townsville	3237	5374	2055	1578	1295	3770	341	2582	1306	2479	4893	3155	5349	2293	
Uluru	1559	3620	441	1617	2290	3012	2837	2931	3802	1935	3139	2287	3595	2804	2496

	Bicheno	Cradle Mountain	Devonport	Hobart	Launceston
Cradle Mountain	383				
Devonport	283	100			
Hobart	186	296	334		
Launceston	178	205	105	209	
Queenstown	443	69	168	257	273

These are the shortest distances by road; other routes may be considerably longer.
For distances by coach, check the companies' leaflets.

note of any numbers to call at the tollpoints to make sure you don't get hit with a fine for late payment – you usually have between one and three days to make any payment.

ROAD RULES

Give way An important road rule is 'give way to the right' – if an intersection is unmarked (unusual) and at roundabouts, you must give way to vehicles entering the intersection from your right.

Speed limits The general speed limit in built-up and residential areas is 50km/h. Near schools, the limit is usually 25km/h (sometimes 40km/h) in the morning and afternoon. On the highway it's usually 100km/h or 110km/h; in the NT it's either 110km/h or 130km/h. Police have speed radar guns and cameras and are fond of using them in strategic locations.

Seatbelts and car seats It's the law to wear seatbelts in the front and back seats; you're likely to get a fine if you don't. Small children must be belted into an approved safety seat.

Drink-driving Random breath-tests are common. If you're caught with a blood-alcohol level of more than 0.05% expect a fine and the loss of your licence. Police can randomly pull any driver over for a breathalyser or drug test.

Mobile phones Using a mobile phone while driving is illegal in Australia (excluding hands-free technology).

FUEL

Fuel types Unleaded and diesel fuel is available from service stations sporting well-known international brand names. LPG (liquefied petroleum gas) is not always stocked at more remote roadhouses; if you're on gas it's safer to have dual-fuel capacity.

Costs Prices vary from place to place, but at the time of writing unleaded was hovering between $1.20 and $1.50 in the cities. Out in the country, prices soar.

Availability In cities and towns petrol stations proliferate, but distances between fill-ups can be long in the outback. That said, there are only a handful of tracks where you'll require a long-range fuel tank. On main roads there'll be a small town or roadhouse roughly every 150km to 200km. Many petrol stations, but not all, are open 24 hours.

SAFETY

Theft from vehicles can be an issue in large cities or tourist areas, but the risk is unlikely to be any higher than you'd encounter back home.

Animal Hazards

➡ Roadkill is a huge problem in Australia and many Australians avoid travelling once the sun drops because of the risks posed by nocturnal animals on the roads.

➡ Kangaroos are common on country roads, as are cows and sheep in the unfenced outback. Kangaroos are most active around dawn and dusk and often travel in groups: if you see one hopping across the road, slow right down, as its friends may be just behind it.

➡ If you hit and kill an animal while driving, pull it off the road, preventing the next car from having a potential road accident. If the animal is only injured and is small, or perhaps an orphaned joey (baby kangaroo), wrap it in a towel or blanket and call the relevant wildlife rescue line:

Wildlife Victoria (☑1300 094 535; www.wildlifevictoria.org.au).

Behind the Wheel

Fatigue Be wary of driver fatigue; driving long distances (particularly in hot weather) can be utterly exhausting. Falling asleep at the wheel is not uncommon. On a long haul, stop and rest every two hours or so – do some exercise, change drivers or have a coffee.

Road trains Be careful overtaking road trains (trucks with two or three trailers stretching for as long as 50m); you'll need distance and plenty of speed. On single-lane roads get right off the road when one approaches.

Unsealed roads Unsealed road conditions vary wildly and cars perform differently when braking and turning on dirt. Don't exceed 80km/h on dirt roads; if you go faster you won't have time to respond to a sharp turn, stock on the road or an unmarked gate or cattle grid.

DRIVING IN OUTBACK AUSTRALIA

In 'Power & the Passion', Midnight Oil's damning ode to the Australian suburban condition, Peter Garrett sings, '*And no-one goes outback that's that.*' It really is amazing how few Australians have explored the outback. To many, it's either a mythical place inhabited by tourists and Indigenous Australians, or something for the too-hard basket – too hot, too far to drive, too expensive to fly, too many sand dunes and flies... But for those that make the effort,

Type of Vehicle

2WD Depending on where you want to travel, a regulation 2WD vehicle might suffice. They're cheaper to hire, buy and run than 4WDs and are more readily available. Most are fuel efficient, and easy to repair and sell. Downsides: no off-road capability and no room to sleep!

4WD Four-wheel drives are good for outback travel as they can access almost any track you get a hankering for. And there might even be space to sleep in the back. Downsides: poor fuel economy, awkward to park and more expensive to hire/buy.

Campervan Creature comforts at your fingertips: sink, fridge, cupboards, beds, kitchen and space to relax. Downsides: slow and often not fuel-efficient, not great on dirt roads and too big for nipping around the city.

Motorcycle The Australian climate is great for riding, and bikes are handy in city traffic. Downsides: Australia isn't particularly bike-friendly in terms of driver awareness, there's limited luggage capacity, and exposure to the elements.

Driving Problem-Buster

What should I do if my car breaks down? Call the service number of your car-hire company and a local garage will be contacted.

What if I have an accident? Your first call should be to the insurance company and you should make sure that you have the contact details (at the very least) of the drivers of all other vehicles involved. Never admit fault unless instructed to do so by your insurance company. For minor accidents you'll need to fill out an accident statement when you return the vehicle. If problems crop up, go to the nearest police station.

What should I do if I get stopped by the police? The police will want to see your driving licence, passport (if you're from overseas) and proof of insurance.

What if I can't find anywhere to stay? If you're travelling during summer and/or holiday periods, always book accommodation in advance as beds fill up fast. If you're stuck and it's getting late, motels and motor inns line the roadside in even small Australian towns, while in outback areas the nearest roadhouse (a one-stop shop for accommodation, food and fuel) is likely to be your only option.

a strange awakening occurs – a quiet comprehension of the primal terrain and profound size of Australia that you simply can't fathom while sitting on Bondi Beach.

About the Outback

The Australian outback is vast, blanketing the centre of the continent. While most Australians live on the coast, that thin green fringe of the continent is hardly typical of this enormous land mass. Inland is the desert soul of Australia.

Weather patterns vary from region to region – from sandy arid deserts to semi-arid scrublands to tropical savannah – but you can generally rely on hot sunny days, starry night skies and mile after mile of unbroken horizon.

Outback Driving & Safety Checklist

You need to be particularly organised and vigilant when travelling in the outback, especially on remote sandy tracks, due to the scorching temperatures, long distances between fuel stops and isolation. Here are a few tips:

Communication

➡ Report your route and schedule to the police, a friend or relative.

➡ Mobile phones are practically useless in the outback. A safety net is to hire a satellite phone, high-frequency (HF) radio transceiver equipped to pick up the Royal Flying Doctor Service bases,

or emergency position-indicating radio beacon (EPIRB).

➡ In an emergency, stay with your vehicle; it's easier to spot than you are, and you won't be able to carry a heavy load of water very far. Don't sit inside your vehicle as it will become an oven in hot weather.

➡ If you do become stranded, set fire to a spare tyre (let the air out first). The pall of smoke will be visible for miles.

Dirt-Road Driving

➡ Inflate your tyres to the recommended levels for the terrain you're travelling on; on desert dirt, deflate your tyres to 25psi to avoid punctures.

➡ Reduce speed on unsealed roads, as traction is decreased and braking distances increase.

➡ Dirt roads are often corrugated: keeping an even speed is the best approach.

➡ Dust on outback roads can obscure your vision, so always stop and wait for it to settle.

➡ If your vehicle is struggling through deep sand, deflating your tyres a bit will help. If you do get stuck, don't attempt to get out by revving the engine; this just causes wheels to dig in deeper.

Road Hazards

➡ Outback highways are usually long, flat ribbons of tarmac stretching across the red desert flats. The temptation is to get it over with quickly, but try to keep a lid on your speed.

121

➡ Take a rest every few hours: driver fatigue is a real problem.

➡ Wandering cattle, sheep, emus, kangaroos, camels, etc make driving fast a dangerous prospect. Take care and avoid nocturnal driving, as this is often when native animals come out. Many car-hire companies prohibit night-time driving.

➡ Road trains are an ever-present menace on the main highways. Give them a wide berth, they're much bigger than you!

Supplies & Equipment

➡ Always carry plenty of water: in warm weather allow 5L per person per day and an extra amount for the radiator, carried in several containers.

➡ Bring plenty of food in case of a breakdown.

➡ Carry a first-aid kit, a good set of maps, a torch and spare batteries, a compass, and a shovel for digging if you get bogged.

Weather & Road Conditions

➡ Check road conditions before travelling: roads that are passable in the Dry (March to October) can disappear beneath water during the Wet.

➡ Check weather forecasts daily.

➡ Keep an eye out for potholes, rough sections, roads changing surfaces without notice, soft and broken verges, and single-lane bridges.

➡ Take note of the water-level markers at creek crossings to gauge the water's depth before you proceed.

➡ Don't attempt to cross flooded bridges or causeways unless you're sure of the depth, and of any road damage hidden underwater.

Your Vehicle

➡ Have your vehicle serviced and checked before you leave.

➡ Load your vehicle evenly, with heavy items inside and light items on the roof rack.

➡ Check locations and opening times of service stations, and carry spare fuel and provisions; opportunities for fill-ups can be infrequent.

➡ Carry essential tools: a spare tyre (two if possible), a fan belt and a radiator hose, as well as a tyre-pressure gauge and an air pump.

➡ An off-road jack might come in handy, as will a snatchem strap or tow rope for quick extraction when you're stuck (useful if there's another vehicle to pull you out).

➡ A set of cheap, high-profile tyres (around $80 each) will give your car a little more ground clearance.

Road Trains

On many outback highways you'll see thundering road trains: huge trucks (a prime mover plus two or three trailers) up to 50m long. These things don't move over for anyone, and it's like a scene out of *Mad Max* having one bear down on you at 120km/h. When you see a road train approaching on a narrow bitumen road, slow down and pull over – if the truck has to put its wheels off the road to pass you, the resulting barrage of stones will almost certainly smash your windscreen. When trying to overtake one, allow plenty of room (about a kilometre) to complete the manoeuvre. Road trains throw up a lot of dust on dirt roads, so if you see one coming it's best to just pull over and stop until it's gone past.

And while you're on outback roads, don't forget to give the standard bush wave to oncoming drivers – it's simply a matter of lifting the index finger off the steering wheel to acknowledge your fellow motorist.

BEHIND THE SCENES

SEND US YOUR FEEDBACK

We love to hear from travellers – your comments help make our books better. We read every word, and we guarantee that your feedback goes straight to the authors. Visit **lonelyplanet.com/contact** to submit your updates and suggestions.

Note: We may edit, reproduce and incorporate your comments in Lonely Planet products such as guidebooks, websites and digital products, so let us know if you don't want your comments reproduced or your name acknowledged. For a copy of our privacy policy visit lonelyplanet.com/privacy.

ACKNOWLEDGMENTS

Climate map data adapted from Peel MC, Finlayson BL & McMahon TA (2007) 'Updated World Map of the Köppen-Geiger Climate Classification', *Hydrology and Earth System Sciences*, 11, 163344.

Cover photographs: Front: Great Ocean Road, near Lorne, Peter Walton Photography/Getty; Back: Tidal River, Wilsons Promontory National Park, Pete Seaward/Lonely Planet ©

THIS BOOK

This 1st edition of *Coastal Victoria Road Trips* was researched and written by Anthony Ham. This guidebook was produced by the following:

Destination Editor Tasmin Waby

Product Editor Amanda Williamson

Assisting Editor Ross Taylor

Senior Cartographers David Kemp, Julie Sheridan

Assisting Cartographer Rachel Imeson

Book Designer Wibowo Rusli

Cover Researcher Campbell McKenzie

Thanks to Kate Chapman, Indra Kilfoyle, Anne Mason, Katherine Marsh, Kate Mathews, Catherine Naghten, Martine Power, Mazzy Prinsep

OUR STORY

A beat-up old car, a few dollars in the pocket and a sense of adventure. In 1972 that's all Tony and Maureen Wheeler needed for the trip of a lifetime – across Europe and Asia overland to Australia. It took several months, and at the end – broke but inspired – they sat at their kitchen table writing and stapling together their first travel guide, *Across Asia on the Cheap*. Within a week they'd sold 1500 copies. Lonely Planet was born.

Today, Lonely Planet has offices in Melbourne, London and Oakland, with more than 600 staff and writers. We share Tony's belief that 'a great guidebook should do three things: inform, educate and amuse'.

INDEX

A

accommodation 13, *see also individual locations*
activities, *see individual activities, locations*
AFL Grand Final 65
Anglesea 20, 81
animals, *see individual species*
Apollo Bay 21, 83-4
archaeological sites 92
art galleries, *see galleries*
Art Gallery of Ballarat 113
Arthurs Seat 41
Arts Centre Melbourne 57
Australian Formula One Grand Prix 65
Australian Open 64

B

Ballarat 49, 111-15, **112**
Baw Baw National Park 98
beaches
  Angelsea 81
  Bells Beach 20, 80
  Fingal Beach 104
  Gibson Steps 85
  Mornington 37, 99
  Ninety-Mile Beach 32
  Phillip Island 90

000 Map pages

Point Addis 20, 80
Squeaky Beach 30, 96
Sorrento 100-1
Torquay 19
Warrnambool 86
beer, *see breweries*
Bells Beach 20, 80
Birregurra 21
Blackwood 48
boat tours
  Melbourne 65
  Nelson 25
  Phillip Island 92
  Sorrento 101
boat travel 38
Booktown Book Fair 48
Boxing Day Test 66
Brae 21
breweries
  Carlton & United 61
  Holgate Brewhouse 106
  Red Hill Breweries 41
Buckley, William 100
budgeting 13
Bunurong Marine & Coastal Park 30
business hours 13

C

canoeig, *see kayaking*
Cape Bridgewater 25
Cape Otway 21, 23, 84
car hire 12, 117-18

car insurance 117
car travel, *see driving*
Castlemaine 46-7, 107-9
caves 25
cell phones 12
climate 12
Clunes 48-9
Coal Creek Village 94
Coiltek Gold Centre 48
cooking schools 29
costs 13
cricket 66

D

diving & snorkelling
  Bunurong Marine & Coastal Park 92
  Inverloch 29
  Portsea 38-9, 103
driving 117-22
  car hire 12, 117-18
  driving licences 117
  fuel 12, 119-20
  insurance 117
  maps 118
  parking 11
  road rules 119
  safety 118-19, 120, 122
  websites 118

E

emergencies 12
Erskine Falls 21

Eureka Skydeck 57
Eureka Stockade 114
events, see festivals & events

F

festivals & events, see also sporting events
Begonia Festival 113-14
Booktown Book Fair 48
Budburst 107
Castlemaine State Festival 108
Falls Festival 20
Festival of Gardens 108
Highland Gathering 110
Kyneton Daffodil & Arts Festival 107
Maldon Folk Festival 110
Melbourne 64-6
Port Fairy Folk Festival 20
Federation Square 52
Flinders 39-40, 104
Flinders Street Station 53
food 13, see also individual locations
football 65
Fort Nepean 105
Fort Queenscliff 38
French Island 41, 104-5
fuel 12, 119-20

G

galleries, see also musems
Art Gallery of Ballarat 113
Australian Centre for Contemporary Art 57
Castlemaine Art Gallery & Historical Museum 108
Centre for Contemporary Photography 61
Ian Potter Centre: NGV Australia 52-3
Mornington Peninsula Regional Gallery 99

NGV International 57
gardens, see parks & gardens
gas 12, 119-20
Gippsland region 27-33, **28-9**
gold mine tours
Carman's Tunnel 110
Long Tunnel Extended Gold Mine 32, 98
gold panning 48
gold rushes 108
Goldfields region 43-9, 106-15, **44-5**
golf courses 20, 102
Great Ocean Road region 17-25, 79-89, **18-19**

H

Hanging Rock 45-6, 106-7
highlights 6-7, 8-9, **6-7**
horse racing 66
horse riding
Mornington Peninsula National Park 104
Warrnambool 86

I

insurance 117
internet access 12
Inverloch 29

K

kangaroos 20, 83
kayaking
Anglesea 81
Apollo Bay 21
Lorne 82
Melbourne 62
Mornington 100
Portsea 103
Kennett River 21
kitesurfing 64
koalas 21, 41, 83, 91

Koonwarra 29-30, 93
Korumburra 93-4
Kryal Castle 113
Kyneton 46, 107

L

lighthouses
Cape Otway 23, 84
Cape Schanck 104
Loch Ard Gorge 24
Logan's Beach whale-watching platform 24, 87
London Bridge, Great Ocean Road 24, 85
London Bridge, Portsea 103
Lorne 20-1, 81-3

M

Macedon 44
Maldon 47-8, 109-10
markets
Collingwood Children's Farm Farmers Market 58
Koonwarra Farmers Market 29-30
Mill Markets 115
Mornington Street Market 99
Queen Victoria Market 56
Red Hill 41
Maryborough 48, 110-11
MCG 61
Melbourne 10-11, 52-78, **54-5, 58-9, 63**
accommodation 10, 66-7
activities 62, 64
drinking & nightlife 71-4
entertainment 74-6
festivals & events 64-6
food 10, 68-71
parking 11
shopping 76-7
sights 52-3, 56-7, 60-2
tours 61, 64

Melbourne *continued*
  travel to/from 13
  travel within 10-11
  walks 63
Melbourne Cricket
  Ground (MCG) 61
Melbourne Cup 66
Melbourne Star 57-8
mobile phones 12
money 13
Mornington 36-7, 99-100
Mornington Peninsula 35-41,
  99-105, **36-7**
Mornington Peninsula
  National Park 39, 103-4
motorcycles, *see* driving
motorsports 65, 91, 92
Museum of Australian
  Democracy at Eureka 113
museums, *see also* galleries
  Australian Centre for the
    Moving Image 53
  Castlemaine Art Gallery &
    Historical Museum 108
  Coal Creek Village 94
  Flagstaff Hill Maritime
    Village 24-5
  Great Ocean Road National
    Heritage Centre 21
  Gold Museum 113
  History of Motorsport
    Museum 91
  Immigration Museum 56
  Kyneton Historical
    Museum 46
  Melbourne Museum 61
  Museum of Australian
    Democracy at Eureka 113
  National Sports
    Museum 61
  Old Treasury Building 53
  Polly Woodside 57
  Sorrento Museum 101

Surf World Museum 79
Walhalla Historical
  Museum 97
Worsley Cottage 110

N

national parks & reserves,
  see also parks & gardens
  Baw Baw National Park 98
  Bunurong Marine &
    Coastal Park 30
  Lower Glenelg
    National Park 25
  Mornington Peninsula
    National Park 39, 103-4
  Point Nepean
    National Park 105
  Port Campbell National
    Park 84-5
  Wilsons Promontory
    National Park 30, 94-7
Nelson 25
Ninety Mile Beach 32
Nobbies, the 91

O

Old Melbourne Gaol 56
opening hours 13

P

parking 11
parks & gardens, *see also*
  national parks & reserves
  Birrarung Marr 53
  Castlemaine Botanical
    Gardens 108
  Garden of St Erth 48
  Kyneton Botanic
    Gardens 46
  Mornington Botanical
    Rose Gardens 99
  Royal Botanic Gardens 62
Parliament House 53
penguins 24, 83, 90

petrol 12, 119-20
Phillip Island 28-9, 90-3, **91**
platypuses 83
Point Addis 20, 80
Point Nepean
  National Park 105
Port Albert 30
Port Campbell 24, 85-6
Port Campbell
  National Park 84-5
Port Fairy 25, 87-9
Port Fairy Folk Festival 20
Portland 89
Portsea 38-9, 103

Q

Queen Victoria Market 56
Queenscliff 38
Queenscliff–Sorrento
  Ferry 38

R

railways
  Victorian Goldfields
    Railway 108, 110
  Mornington Railway 100
  Walhalla Goldfields
    Railway 98
Red Hill 41
reserves, *see* national
  parks & reserves
Rip Curl Pro 80
river cruises
  Melbourne 64
  Nelson 25
road distances
  Australia 119
  Great Ocean Road 89
road rules 119
Royal Botanic Gardens 62
Royal Exhibition Building 62
Royal Melbourne Zoo 62

000 Map pages

S

safety 118-19, 120, 122
Seal Rocks 91
seals 91
Seaspray 32
Shipwrecked 25
shipwrecks 88
Shrine of Remembrance 62
snorkelling, *see*
  diving & snorkelling
Sorrento 37, 100-3
Sovereign Hill 111, 113
sporting events, *see also*
  festivals & events
  AFL Grand Final 65
  Australian Formula One
    Grand Prix 65
  Australian Motorcycle
    Grand Prix 92
  Australian Open 64, 76
  Boxing Day Test 66
  Melbourne Cup 66
  Pier to Pub Swim 82
  Rip Curl Pro 20, 80
Squeaky Beach 30
St Patrick's Cathedral 57
St Paul's Cathedral 53
strawberry picking 41
surfing
  Anglesea 81
  Inverloch 29
  Mornington Peninsula
    National Park 104
  Phillip Island 92
  Port Fairy 87
  Torquay 20, 79-80

T

telephone services 12
tennis 64, 76
Tidal River 94
tipping 13

toll roads 118-19
Torquay 19-20, 79-80
tourist offices 11, *see also*
  individual locations
tours, *see also* boat tours,
  gold mine tours, river
  cruises, walking tours,
  individual locations
  breweries 58
  canoeing 25
  caves 25
  diving 39, 103
  dolphin swimming 37
  ghosts 98, 113
  Grand Prix Circuit 91
  helicopter rides 24
  horse riding 86
  kayaking 21
  MCG 61
  penguin watching 90
  river cruises 25, 64
  seals 21, 25, 37
  shipwrecks 21
  wineries 44, 81, 103
transport 13, 116-22
travel seasons 12
Trentham 48
Twelve Apostles 23-4, 85

V

Victorian Goldfields Railway
  Castlemaine 108
  Maldon 110
  Walhalla 98

W

Walhalla 32, 97-8
walking tours
  Apollo Bay 21
  Lorne 81-2
  Melbourne 63, 64, **63**
  Port Fairy 87
  Portland 89

Wilsons Promontory 96
wallabies 83
Warrnambool 24-5, 86-8
weather 12
websites 11, 118
whale watching 83, 87
wi-fi 12
wildlife, *see* zoos & wildlife
  reserves, *individual*
  species
Wilsons Promontory
  National Park 94-7, **95**
wineries
  Basalt Wines 25
  Lyre Bird Hill Winery 93
  Macedon 44
  Montalto 104
  Port Phillip Estate 103
Red Hill Estate 103
  Ten Minutes by Tractor 103
  T'Gallant 103
Woodend 45-6, 106

Z

zoos & wildlife reserves
  Ballarat Wildlife Park 113
  Koala Conservation
    Centre 91
  Penguin Parade 90
  Royal Melbourne Zoo 62

OUR WRITER

ANTHONY HAM

Anthony (www.anthonyham.com) was born in Melbourne, grew up in Sydney and spent much of his adult life travelling the world. He recently returned to Australia after ten years living in Madrid and brings to this guide more than fifteen years' experience as a travel writer. As a recently returned expat, Anthony is loving the opportunity to rediscover his country and indulge his passion for the wilderness. He brings to the book the unique perspective of knowing the land intimately and yet seeing it anew as if through the eyes of an outsider.

Published by Lonely Planet Publications Pty Ltd
ABN 36 005 607 983
1st edition – Nov 2015
ISBN 978 1 74360 943 9
© Lonely Planet 2015   Photographs © as indicated 2015
10 9 8 7 6 5 4 3 2 1
Printed in China